I0103336

A Glimmer of Hope:
Rocky's Story

by Michelle Brown

~ A Glimmer of Hope ~

This book is dedicated to my mum for all her
emotional and financial support throughout
Rocky's recovery.

To all Rocky's friends—past and present—who
have touched both our lives which has brought us
to this point in life.

To Rocky: for being part of my life, giving me a
purpose, being my best friend, for his
unconditional love, making me laugh, sometimes
cry. For being a fighter and the character he is.

~ A Glimmer of Hope ~

First published in the United Kingdom 2011.

Cover Design © Plan4 Media
Horse Shoe Graphics © Tribalium 81

Photographs © Taken by: Michelle Brown, Francis and Paul Ockford, Christine Walker, Debbie White & Mark Baxter

A catalogue record of this book is available from the British Library

ISBN: 978-1-907463-44-0

Contents

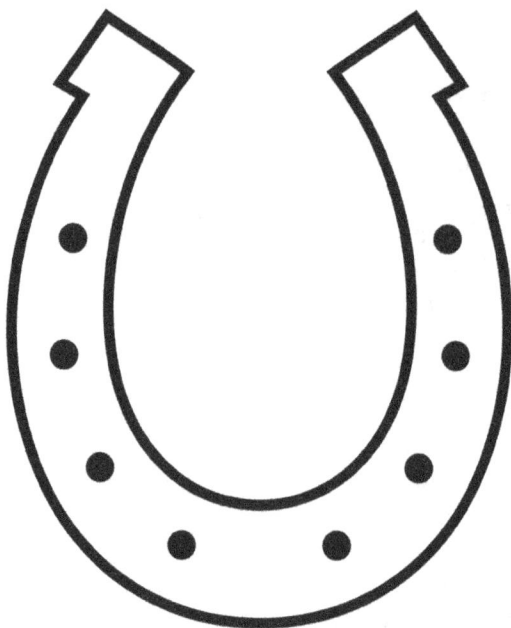

Introduction

This story is about a young race horse that was trained as a two-year-old but un-raced then sold on into a life of neglect that was rescued by a person who was at the time in emotional need themselves and together working their way through life. Sharing the true life experiences: of the horse's pain, the hope, the ups and downs, the risks and love when most would have given up on him as a lost cause. When all the hard work, training, justice, love and care for him to turn about, as he is chosen to star in movie which then opens new doors as a documentary about his life: his neglect and raise to stardom is made.

One

On September 5th 2008, I was asked by a work colleague, I also knew outside of work, if I wanted to buy a 16'1" four-year-old thoroughbred bay gelding ex-race horse. It was going cheap because he had a bit of rain scald.

I had been without a horse since joining the civil service in September 2002. As a child I had worked mucking out, grooming, breaking in ponies, going to local shows; once the pony was good enough and winning competitions—it was sold. That was always the hardest part; working and bonding with the ponies emotionally then them being sold. As I was what some would call a *loner* as a child, I didn't have real friends or socialise outside of school because I was always working. I learnt from a young age to trust animals as they don't hurt you like people can. I left home and went to an agricultural college where I gained horse qualifications. I ended up in a catering job like most students; you take whatever jobs are available. I was offered a job working with horses in Germany for six months, which I took, that was an experience I shall never forget, farriers make you hold the leg up whilst they shoe the horse.

When I returned to England I worked with horses as a groom for polo ponies, hunters, show jumpers, I taught others to ride, I used to break in/school young or problem horses. I brought my own youngsters to bring on as this is what I knew best and enjoyed doing.

There is something special about bringing on and

gaining the trust of a young or frightened horse. I have always had my own tactics for gaining trust and bonding with horses, of course it doesn't always go right but despite the bites, the kicks, the falls and being bolted with meaning the horse gallops off whilst your riding it and you have no control until the horse calms down.

So horses have always been in my life since I was a young child. Due to a non horse-related accident I had to give them up for a while, and find what some people consider a *proper job*, but horses are in my blood and heart. So I decided to go see this horse.

When I arrived with my colleague and ex-partner at the time, the horse was out in the field so I went with the chap selling him to get the horse in, just so I could see what he was like to catch. Well, my heart sank because although rugged up in a torn wet rug he was clearly finding it hard to move let alone walk in from the field. The chap said it was the missing shoe causing him to be so slow.

I first noticed the open wounds on two of his legs, not cleaned or treated. When I got the rug removed I was dismayed and my ex-partner was distressed to see what was standing in front of us. My colleague whispered she had no idea the rain scald was so bad, the rain scald covered the poor horse from nose to tail, he was scabs and bone, with several open cuts.

Rain scald is a bacterial skin disease horses can get from being in wet conditions for prolonged periods, having minor wounds and being in contact with other horses that have the bacterial disease known as *carriers*. Horses with rain scald will generally have clumps of matted hair in the most commonly affected areas such as the neck, saddle area, and loins. In more sever cases horses can have legs and their belly affected where water has run down the body.

Right then my head was saying no but I asked the young man how much? He replied "£2,500". I asked him if the vet had seen the horse. He replied, "Yes." I asked the outcome; the reply I got was unbelievable. According to the chap selling the horse, "Vets don't prescribe anti-biotic for rain scald," even though this case was clearly infected and pussy. I was told by the man the vets posted him steroids to give the horse, which he then went and got from his house. When he came back he showed me the envelope with small steroids in, he stated: "The horse was to have 5 tablets a day." I looked at the tablets with a rough count; it was clear he hadn't even started the horse on the tablets. That's even if they were for the horse. There was no labelling or directions on the medication! I asked which vets had come to see him. The man gave me two equine vets' names; said he couldn't remember which practice came out: I asked if he had been wormed. He said, "Yes, last week." I discussed the situation with my then ex-partner; raising how neglected this horse is and that I shouldn't get him, but the more I looked at him, I felt something, my heart couldn't leave him there—in these conditions. The sad thing was there was ample empty stables, a stack of straw and a stack of hay, no reason for this poor horse to be starving. The horse was placed in a stable and as I was walking away he whickered and I foolishly turned, where I saw a glimmer in his sad eyes. That was it, my was heart stolen. I saw something in him I can't explain what at this time but hopefully you'll all see why later.

I offered the man £400 explaining that the horse is/ was neglected, in need of stabling and a lot care. I know about rain scald and its treatment; however this, in my eyes, was a severe case of rain scald which has been left untreated. Of course, he said no to my offer. I asked why the horse was in such a poor state. He said he had collected the horse in the April 2008 from a local racing yard; he kept it for a bit then sold it to an 11-year-old girl who apparently tried jumping him over 1metre 10 show jumps which the horse refused. She brought it back, put it in the field and it's been there ever since. The man claims he had a black show jumper the girl wanted instead, so they swapped. He claimed the girl must have returned the horse in that state. That he never looked under the rug when it came back.

Today is the first day he has seen him without his rug on. Okay, that's a contradiction I picked up on straight away. Why would he have had the vet to the horse if he hadn't seen the under the horses rug? He also walked up to the horse trying to convince me the scabs on his back are only surface and will pick of easily and started to pick at some, to show me, he obviously had no idea, the horse was clearly in pain and the man pulling the scabs off was hurting him but he was too weak to object, so I nodded at the man as a sign to make him think I believed him in an attempt to make him stop pulling at this poor horse. He did, thank goodness, but he continued to try and explain to me that the scabs will just fall off and nature will take its course.

I could tell the scabs were pussy in some areas and clearly infected. I raised this fact, but the man wasn't having any of it; he just replied, "Well, the vets said it wasn't infected and the steroids will speed up the process of healing." I raised my offer to £800. The man's reply was, "I got a dealer coming tomorrow lunch time, he will give me a grand and load it up on his lorry straight away—no questions asked." I discussed this with my ex-partner and although against my head, told the man, "I will give you a grand cash tomorrow as too late to get to the bank and come back, but the horse must stay in; he needs bedding up and Ab-lib hay and water, the rugs need to come off and stay off to air his back and start him on those tablets if they really are for him," which he assured me they were. I enquired about the missing shoe being replaced. He said he would get his farrier to call, and he would sort the horse out. I asked about his passport which he replied he would find it and give it to me tomorrow.

Because the horse was clearly too weak to travel, I asked if he could he stay here for a week as a livery and I would pay for a stable. We agreed £50 for the stable and the man would give him hay and water every morning. As I was working not far away, I would go in my lunch hour to muck him out and tend to his sores.

I went and stroked the horse, whose name was apparently *Bubbles*, though he didn't know his name. As I rubbed his forehead he lowered his head and pushed his nose into my chest, somehow knowing his suffering was almost over. On our way home I debated over whether I had done the right thing. Anyway, he needed me regardless of the outcome. I have just brought a 4-year-old thoroughbred, I didn't see it ridden or even trot up, how mad am I with all my years of horsemanship? I have never been so reckless or seen such suffering. I rang both vets' practices he gave me to try to validate his claims a vet had seen the horse but neither vets would tell me anything... *"previous owners confidentiality"*, despite telling them I am now the owner of the horse and wanting to know if the horse registered at their practice? Could they confirm whether the horse is on any medication? I couldn't get any answers. I was advised to ask the previous owner to ring the vets, to give his permission to release information, as if he was going to do that—he couldn't even remember which vets had come out to see the horse.

We stopped at feed merchants and tack shop because the horse didn't come with any equipment. I got him a soft head colour, some soft brushes, some simple basic cool mix to introduce to his system, medical kit to tend to his wounds and a new outdoors rug size 6'3". The rug would swamp him although it was the right length. I knew he would need one in case it rained and I was walking him out of his stable as he still needed to stretch his legs, but could not get anymore rain on his already very sore scabby back.

Two
6th September 2008

We arrived at the yard with the money late morning. Whilst I was waiting for the man to come out, I went to see the horse. He was clearly pleased to see me, there was a sparse scattering of shavings on the floor, no hay or water, I was fuming! I gave him hay and water. A girl who was there with her own horse asked if I had bought him. I said yes she was so pleased. I asked if the man had been out, she replied no, no-one has been out since she got there earlier in the morning.

I stated and questioned how come no-one has given this poor horse hay or water or even a decent bed; that I was disgusted, how can anyone walk past and not give him even the basic hay and water? She replied, "It's like that here."

The man appeared. I asked why he hadn't been out to hay the horse. He told me he had been out last night and stayed out. He claims to have asked a local girl to come and feed the horses.

I told him I wanted the horse on a deep straw bed and asked who owned the hay and straw stacks. He said they were his so I said I would be using that whilst the horse is here; that I would be taking him as soon as he is strong enough to travel as the yard I had arranged for him was 30 miles away. I gave him the money, asked for the passport but he said he couldn't find it that he would get a duplicate and send it to me. Once he had counted the money he was gone. My ex-partner and I looked at the horse—now quietly chomping on hay—and decided he needed a new name. We came up with two names: Oliver, because he wanted/needed food, and Rocky, because I believed he was a fighter and could get past this neglect and be a wonderful little horse. I decided to take some photographs of him in his neglected state.

We cleared out the scattering of shavings, and gave him a massive straw bed, a big hay net and some loose on the floor so if the man didn't come out in the morning he would have plenty to be going on with. We gave him three buckets of water to ensure he had enough. I asked the girl who was brushing her own horse, that if she comes down and he doesn't have hay or water please just give him some which she replied yes, of course.

We ended up spending the afternoon with him, making everything right and comfortable for him. I gave him a handful of mix just to start getting feed into his system; we watched him munching through his hay only stopping to drink and on a couple of occasions look up at me. We went home leaving him to eat and rest.

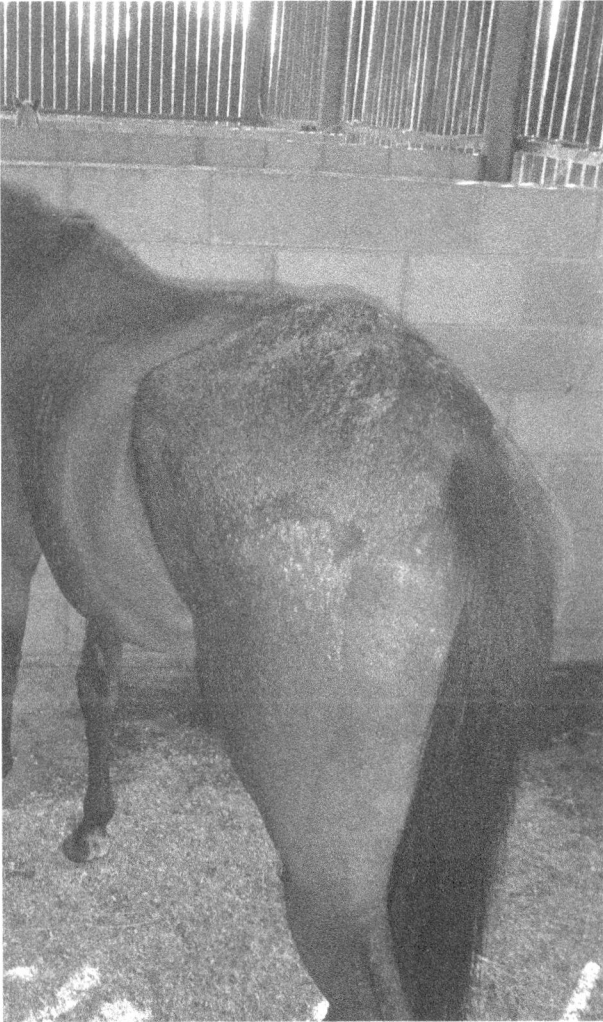

Rocky beginning his healing journey

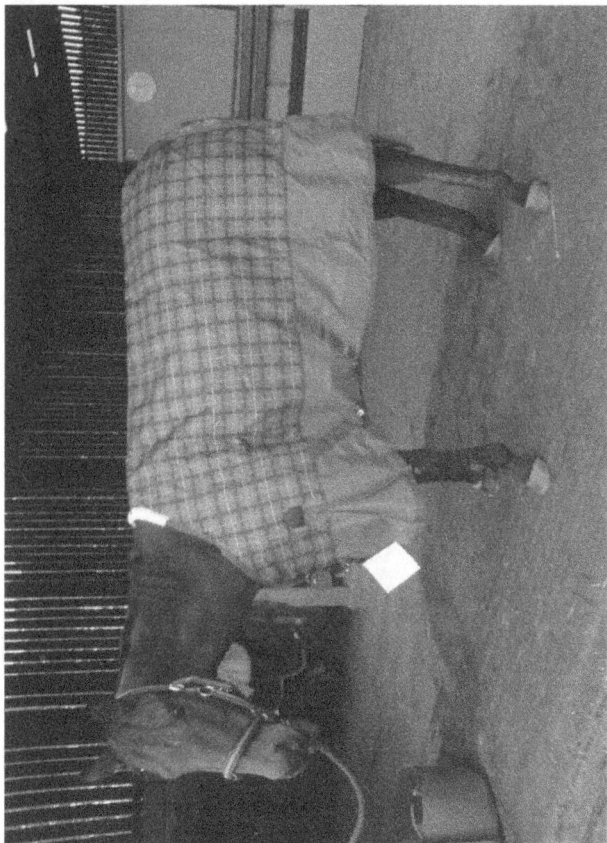

Rocky's comfort blanket

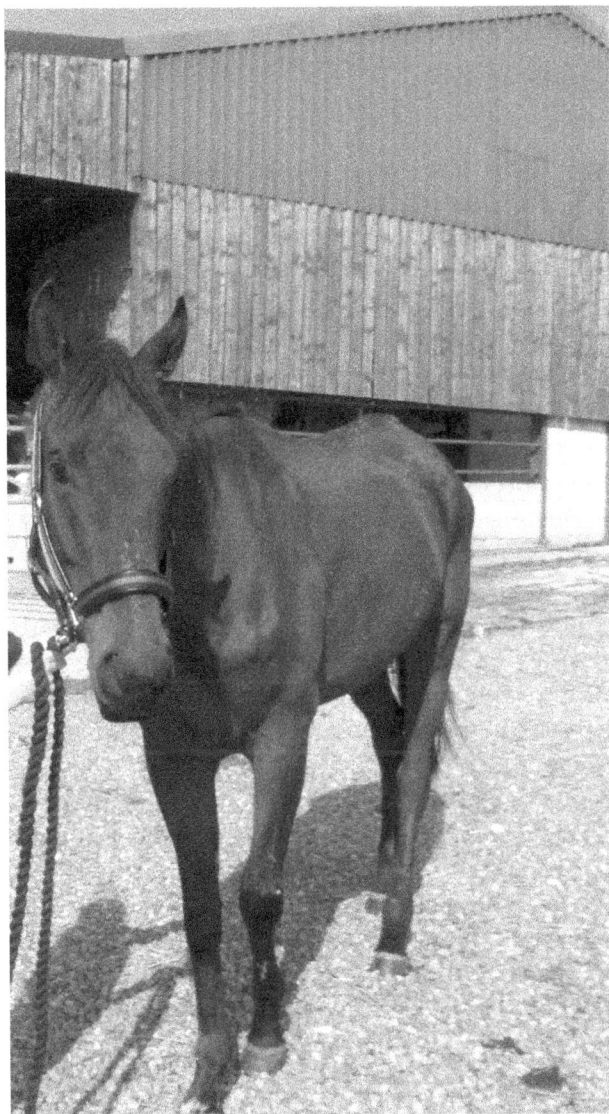

Trusting Rocky

Three
7th September 2008

My life was some what complicated; although I took my ex-partner to see him initially as we still shared a home; although I was sort of seeing someone else. They had a horse. I told them I had bought one so on my day off they came with me to see him. When they saw him I was asked, "What the hell have you bought? What have you done, are you mad?" I replied I couldn't just leave him. He needed me and I felt I needed him. Because my personal life was tearing me apart and as a child I found comfort and solitude in the horses; I didn't care what anyone thought or said about me buying him by this point.

I had the day off work so we went over in the morning to see *Rocky* as that is the name we chose for him. When I pulled up and walked towards his stable his little head popped over the door and he whickered slightly nodding his head. Okay, he knows I'm mum, maybe, or is it he wants food?

He had cleared all the hay we had left for him and he had half a bucket of water left. I hung his hay net but he followed me back to the door. I filled his other hay net and tied it up outside. I led him out of his stable and tied him up with his hay net, as he needed to stretch his legs and more importantly to him, wanted fresh hay. As I was walking away he nuzzled my coat pocket and found carrots, so I let him have some and went to muck out. I spent most of the day with him; we took photos of him, let the sun shine on his back whilst tending to his wounds.

Watching him eat, stroking his face, where there was a small area not covered in scabs. He was so gentle and loving, whether he sensed I was kind or just someone giving him food who knows, but for him to put up with and cope with having deep infected wounds that must have stung like hell cleaned; he must have trusted me and knew I was trying to help him.

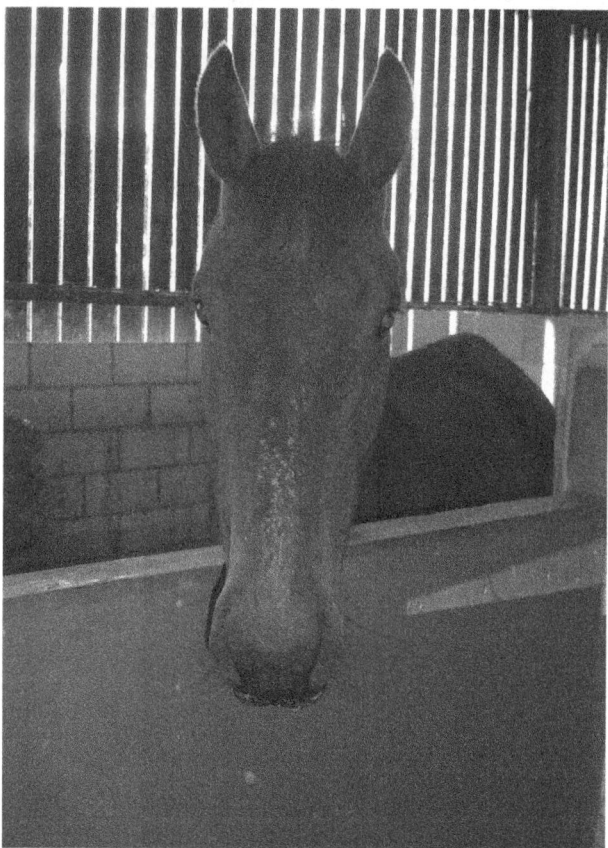

Curious Rocky

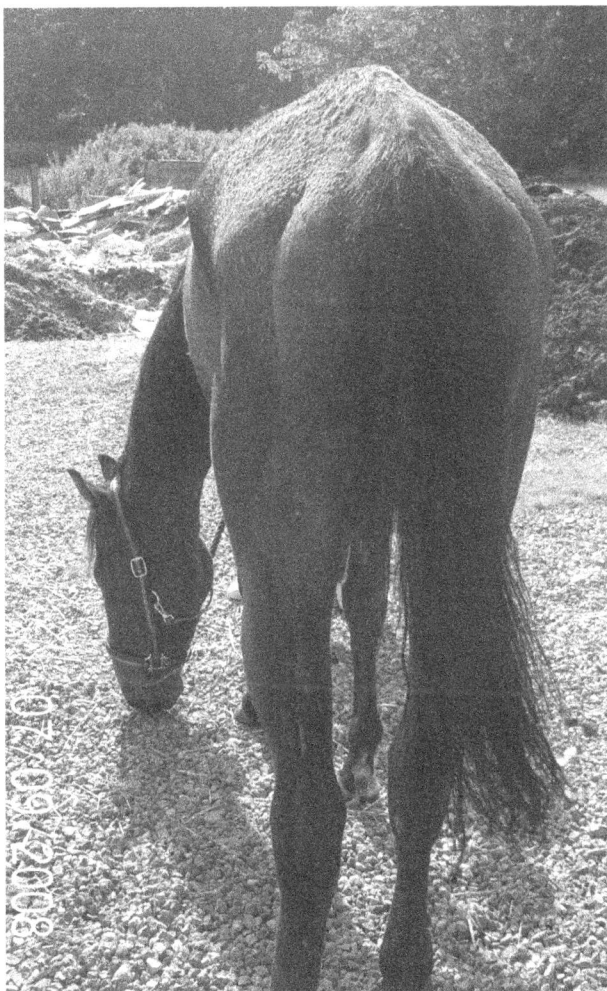

A taste of freedom

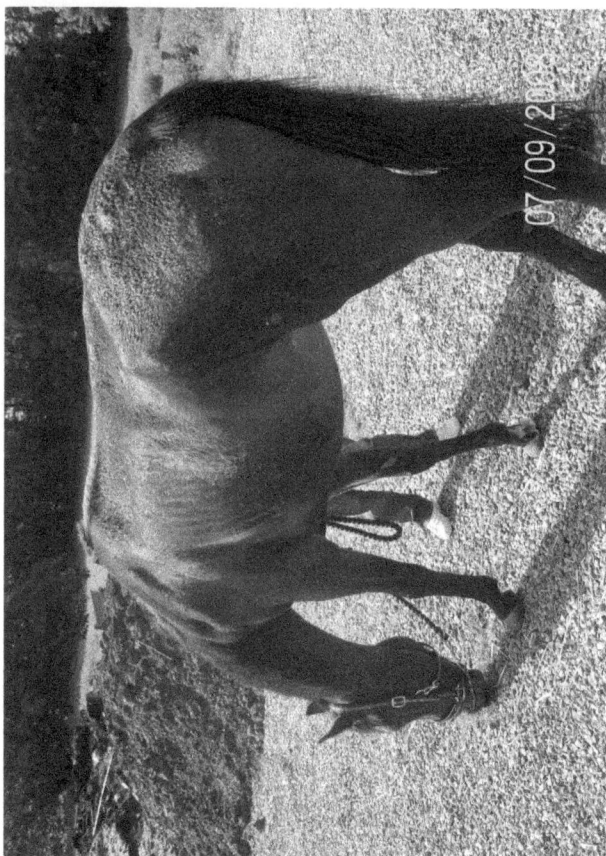

Rocky with some much-needed sun on his back

Four

8th September 2008

I'm back to work happy in the knowledge that I had given Rocky lots of TLC, food and water yesterday and that someone would give him his hay net I left out for him this morning. That I would go see him and muck out at lunch time; well I got to him 12:40 to my upmost horror: his hay net was still full outside his door; his water buckets dry. I hung his hay net, put his fresh water in and gave him a cuddle. *Oops,* no change of clothes, hairy uniform, tough! Nothing matters, trying hard not to let him pick up on the fact I was fuming.

My anger flared and I stormed to the house but got no reply!!

I mucked him out and set off back to work. Work went so slowly, I wasn't finishing until 20:00hrs, but when I finished I went to the stables and gave him a hay net for the night; topped up his bed and water, tended to his wounds knowing I would be down in the morning as I had tomorrow off.

Five

9th September 2008

I went over to see him and tend to his needs. He likes the camera! Once he was all sorted out for the day. I went over to the new yard where he was going to move to speak about the stabling and travelling arrangements. I knew I had to get him off the yard he was at, ASAP.

We got a stable ready for him; he was going to have the end of a set of three stables next door to the horse that would become his friend. I was told the earliest anyone could pick him up would be Thursday 11th September, two days away. Okay, we can both cope for two more days and we did. I never saw the man who sold me Rocky all the time I was at the yard even though he had other horses there.

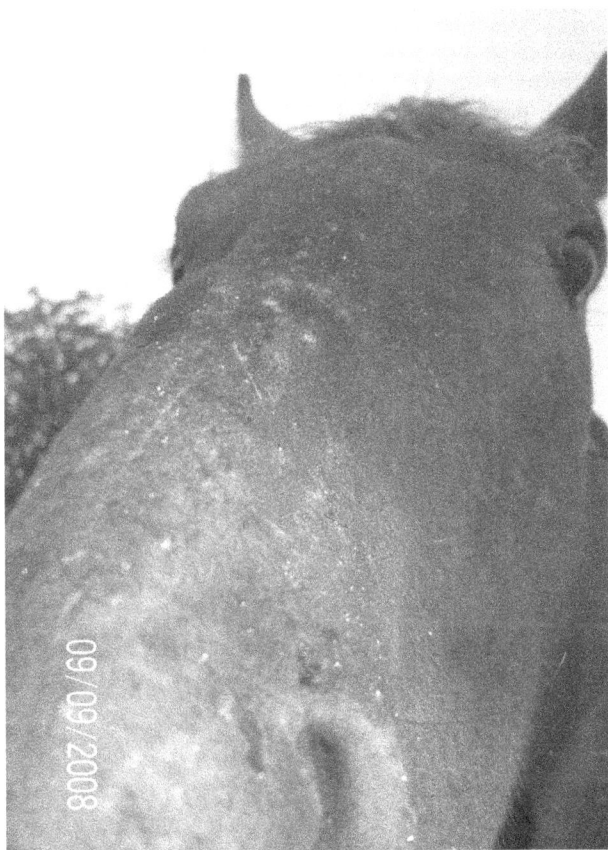

Rocky loves the camera

Six

11th September 2008

I got up early and went over to feed Rocky and muck him out. I drove over to the new yard so I could travel in the lorry to give directions to where he was to collect him. I had already warned the people with me not to be too shocked at the state of him, and I had no idea whether he would load or how he would travel.

We arrived at the yard; the man wasn't around, only one girl tending to her own horse. She asked, "You taking him away?" I said yes, he needed to leave this hell hole where no-one seems to have a heart or give a damn. She asked if the man knew. I said yes, he knows he's going sometime, but he hasn't answered my calls or been on the yard so it's my horse I can do what I want.

My priority was getting Rocky away from there. I prepped him for travel; he didn't mind having travel boots on. We decided not to rug him in case he sweated during travelling; instead we place blankets over the lorry partition to give him some padding as his bones were prominent. I had a carrot in my pocket and bucket of feed just in case he wouldn't load. He walked gingerly up to the lorry, as shock horror his shoe hadn't been replaced. We got to the ramp and I walked up. He stopped at the bottom just looking at me halfway up and he sniffed the ramp so I got the carrot out my pocket, show it to him and he took a couple of steps, so I gave him half the carrot. He then came the rest of the way up the ramp. Bless him, a very good boy, it was quite a slow procedure but I wasn't going to rush him. I got his kit and we were away to his new home, new life.

 His new yard has over thirty-five horses on it ranging from riding school, to hunters, to jousters, stunt and film horses; though at the time none of that entered my head. It's a family-run yard with liveries and at the time a full-time groom. Everyone was dismayed when he was unloaded. Well, I let him have a look around and then put him in his stable where he ate and then promptly laid down and slept.

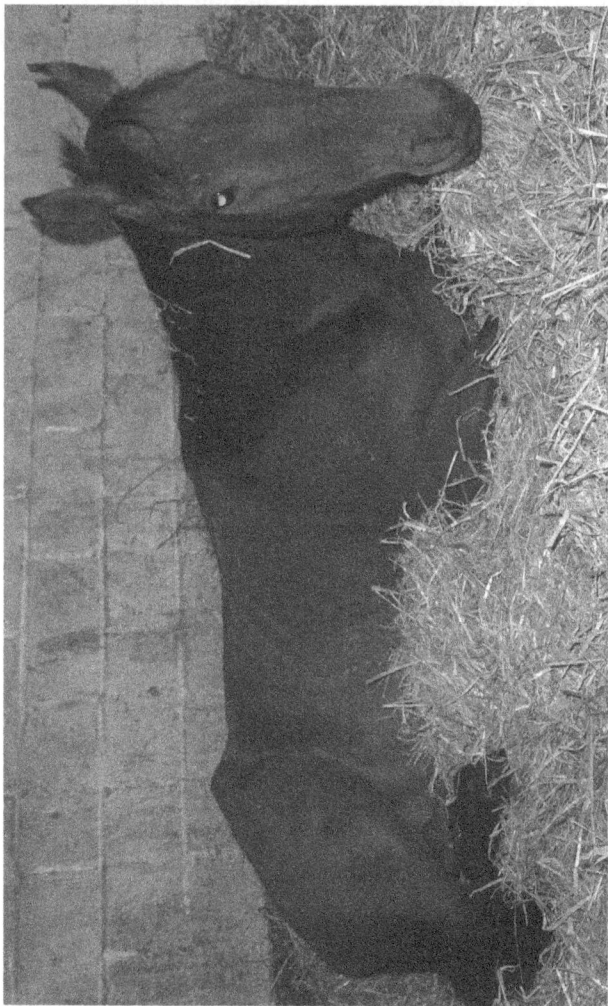

Rocky having a well-deserved rest

Seven

The next day the vet was called out to see him. The vets words were, "I have never seen a case of rain scald and neglect so bad in all my thirty-three years of practising, you must be completely mad to have brought this horse, it will cost a lot for medication. I replied, "I don't care, give him what he needs." The vet said he's a risk and don't be too hopeful he will make it. I know everyone, including the vet, thought this poor little horse should be put down, but I wasn't ready to let that happen, he just needed a chance.

I found some humour in the fact he said he needs immediate injection of anti-biotic for infection, vitamins and controlled diet of hard feed, then a 5-day course of powdered anti-biotic. Considering the comments his previous owner made about the horse not requiring anti-biotic medication and challenging my knowledge of rain scald. Plus he needs to be out in the fresh air without rugs. I was like, "It's cold now, winter is coming." He wasn't allowed to get wet either, so we decided if it was a sunny day he would go out in the day, in at night. He wasn't allowed to sweat either. So much to take in, just how bad this horse really is. He has a lame front leg due to wounds; he's lame both legs behind due to open wounds and missing shoe. I know the general consensus on the yard no-one could see why I brought this horse, when I could have got a fit healthy one for less money if people had known I wanted one. I even believe some thought he wouldn't survive, must admit he had me worried when he got a form of Azoturia aka tied up he was stuck in the field, his system was unfortunately overloaded with injections and good food, his muscles had gone into spasm but the vet came and counter-acted the system overload.

Eight

I contacted the RSPCA and informed them I had brought this neglected horse and wanted to report the previous owner. I was told the previous owner was already known to the RSPCA and had previously been warned about his conduct and lack of care to the animals. As I didn't get his passport I continued to try to contact the man. I wanted him to sign a receipt as proof of sale and proof of my purchase which we would both sign and date; as I knew my vet had reported this matter to the RSPCA; plus I would need it to get a duplicate passport. Eventually after several non-answered calls, I typed up a proof of purchase: I printed it twice and drove to his place but on the way, on a single track lane, I saw him on a vehicle coming towards me so I took up 80% of the road so he had no choice but to stop.

I approached him, told him how much I had already spent in vets bill, and that I was disgusted by his lack of actions and neglect; that I wanted the passport—which he said he didn't have so I said, "Sign the proof of sale and purchase. A copy for each of us and I will get a duplicate done." He signed, reluctantly but he knew I would not move my car until he did so.

After a week on anti-biotic, Rocky wasn't getting any better, so the vet came again and this time prescribed anti-biotic to be administered by injection into his muscles and bless him; as I had to work a full-time job and lived 27 miles away the groom said she would take charge of giving him injections. Just as well, although I can inject inter-muscular; the size of the needle and Rocky being so poor I felt so sorry for him but deep down he must have known we were trying to help him as he just stood there and took it. He didn't object to any treatment done to him, he just stood very still.

Nine

On my days off I would go and see him. The farrier had been and re-shoe'd him; all round he was good to shoe or maybe too weak to protest. As I couldn't ride him or do a lot with him, I would take him for walks up the track to eat the long grass verges, everyone who passed looking with accusing eyes.

I would also sit in his stable with him just watching him eat. On one occasion I sat on the adjoining stable wall, he was in a playful mood, he was playing and licking my Wellington boot; he nibbled the end of my boot and then bit the end and started nodding his head back and forth so I wriggled my toes and my boot came off. He played with it for a bit but then put his head over his door and dropped my boot the other side of the stable door. I thought this was quite funny until I realised I had to go get my boot inside the stable. It was fine as there was lots of fresh straw but outside was raining and he'd managed to get my part of my boot in a puddle. I spent hours watching him eat and drink slowly—he started gaining weight.

The thing with rain scald is the coat continues to grow and covers up the scabs so in appearance and from a distance the hundreds of scabs are not visible. He needed another set of injections of anti-biotic before it started to have an effect. His winter coat started to grow with that the scabs started coming off—revealing a yellow puss on his skin. People at the yard thought—myself included—God, he's going to lose all his coat and it may not grow back. His back was just solid thick scabs, I nick-named *The Armadillo.*

I discussed what to do with the vet. We decided hibi scrub strong solution with warm water so it makes a bubble foam effect and dab all over his back to try and break down some of the scabs whilst he was in this state. It was now winter, no grass turn out, so I would let him run in the school loose with his new friend, the horse next door. They would nuzzle each other in the school and as Rocky got stronger they would gallop around and race each other bucking, rolling, although the school was wet I felt rolling would be good for him and I could clean him up afterwards with the hibi scrub.

I also decided I would spray his back with a wound ointment purple spray. His bottom was just a mass of solid thick hard scabs. Some scabs the size of my hand just slid off, revealing puss, and some blood-spotted skin. I showed others on the yard. Oh dear, they have weak stomachs. I could only compare what I was holding in my hand to what an Indian would hold after scalping someone.

As he was getting more strength and putting weight on I was feeling happy then one day I led him out and his fetlock was not flexing back into position for him to stand, or walk; his stifles had locked. I got underneath his flanks and pushed him up enough to put his hoof back on the floor correctly, now he wasn't moving and he was half out of his stable. Others on the yard came and said I needed the vet. I replied no, I need bandages first. I bandaged both his back legs; one with vet wrap to give maximum support.

Once the bandages were on I pushed him

backwards to free up his stifle and he wandered the rest of the way out freely and turned round and went back in his box. He spent the next month in support bandages.

In late October 2008, whilst out in a paddock with haylage on the ground due to the lack of goodness in the grass at this time of year, he had a small setback as the mares in the next field broke into his paddock and chased him around. He had some nasty cuts on his legs where he got kicked as he wasn't fast enough to run away from them. The groom heard the commotion and went and got him in. His original wound on his back leg had re-opened, this was all due to him being fragile, he had to have deep straw beds as when he laid down and got up he would skin his legs.

Eventually he was well enough to go back in the school for a run around and boy he was full of it after good food and box rest.

Resolute Rocky

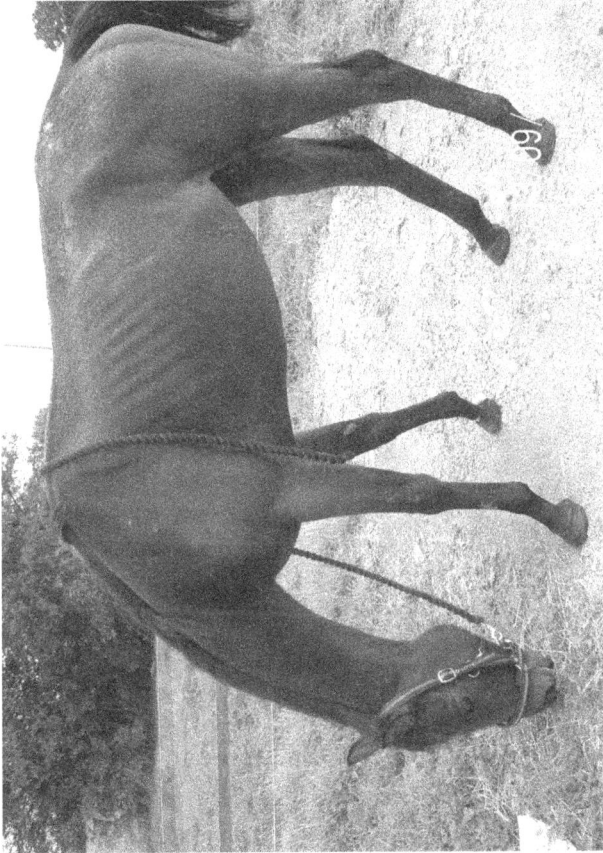

Business as usual for Rocky

Rocky taking it all in his stride

Rocky knows he is in good hands as he makes his
remarkable recovery

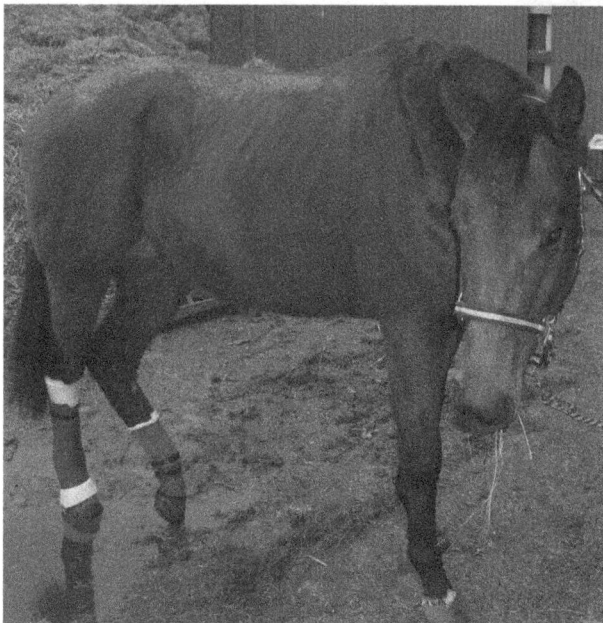

Taking it one step at a time

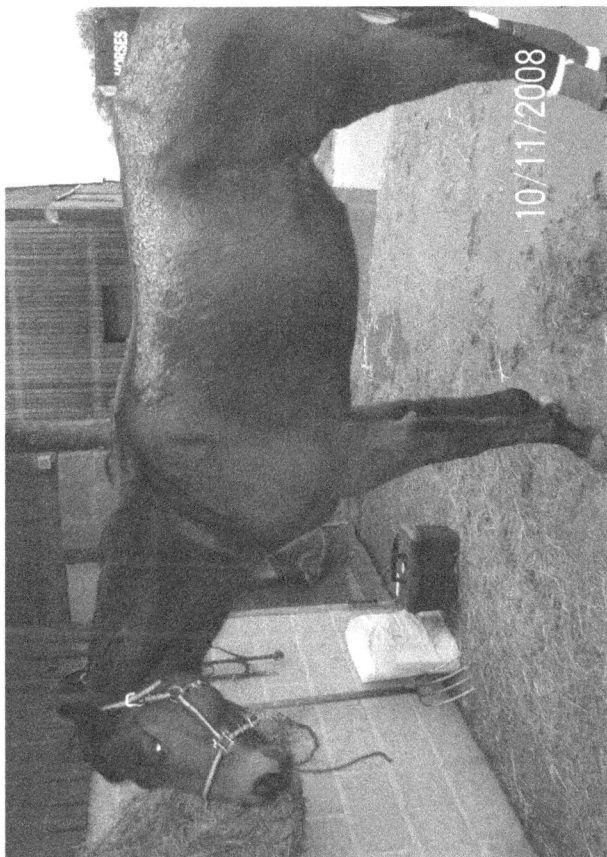

Homely comforts

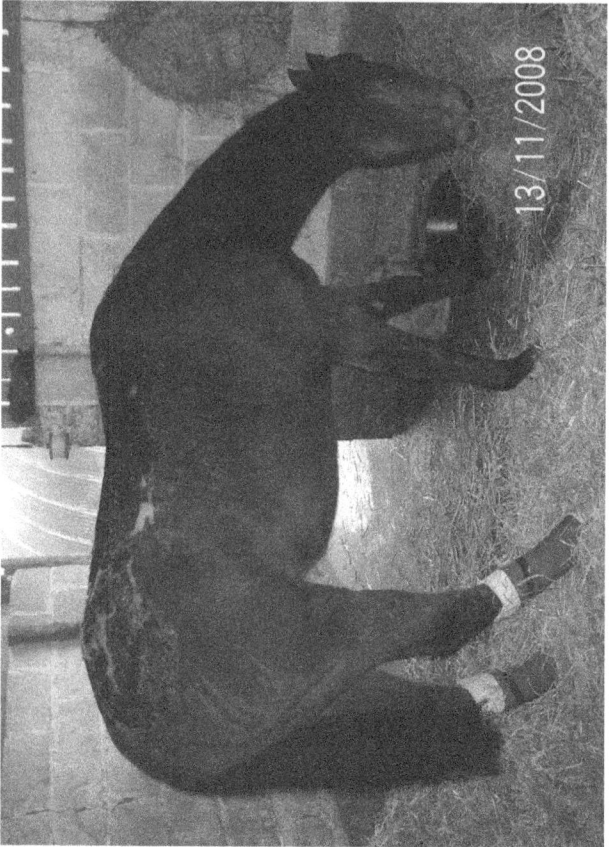

Appetizing Rocky

Rocky growing in confidence each day

Nothing like a bit of show-off time

Ten

Icontacted Whetherbys and explained how I came about this horse and that I know his racing name: *Baron Betts*. That the man who sold him to me failed to get me the passport that I needed a duplicate. That I have a proof of sale receipt. The vet said he is micro-chipped as all race horses get them when born. I was put through to the correct department and explained my circumstances yet again, I was told it was against the law to buy a horse without the passport and your not suppose to travel horses without their passport. I assured them that I had chased the passport but the man I brought him from failed to give it to me and did not appear on the yard the whole time I was there.

  They asked me to send them all the information I had along with the vet certificate and on this occasion would send me a duplicate passport if the documentation was in order. I got all the documentation and marking done and sent away for his passport.

Eleven

Rocky was born 16/02/2005. That made him three-years-old when I brought him, not four, so he was only a baby, not even fully developed in my mind although thoroughbreds mature quicker than some other breeds. When someone attempted to show jump him over big coloured fences no wonder he refused.

Over the next few winter months when home alone on a night, as my so-called new relationship had broken down in a matter of weeks, I'm told through no fault of my own it's just because of other issues, which if I'm truthful although I took it bad at the time was for the best as it allowed me to focus purely on Rocky and my Westies.

My personal life was at rock bottom. I had moved out of the house I jointly owned due to it being impossible to share due to the circumstances. I was living in a caravan and through winter, with frozen pipes, no running water, having bottled water to cook, make drinks and boil a kettle for a wash. I was visiting my mum some 45 miles away once-a-week to do some washing, but I also went to my house to see the two Westies I jointly owned as I couldn't have them with me in the caravan as it was a no pets accommodation. I missed them terribly but whilst visiting them I would do some washing and grab a shower. I would also get to shower at work in the locker rooms; it was a hard time but you make do the best you can. On the plus side I was only living 5 miles away from Rocky so I would see him almost everyday. However this book is about Rocky and his life, I don't like to talk about or express my personal life but all I will add is without Rocky I may have found myself going down a completely unpleasant road of sadness and possible depression due to repeatedly feeling let down and used by other people. People seem to have a natural ability to seek out kind hearted people and drain them of all energy but when the kind hearted person has listened and fixed their problems, their life is fantastic; once again they are nowhere to be found in a time of need. My three boys gave me a reason to get up every morning; they have unconditional love no matter how low you feel: they give cuddles and a purpose in life.

So on the cold wet dark lonesome winter nights I went on the internet to research this ex-race horse. I found his breeding history; he was trained but never raced. I found he came from Ireland as a yearling; he is out of Northern dancer blood line who is a famous Canadian race horse who raced in USA and won. So this little horse is very well bred.

His passport arrived but only had my details and the breeder's details, nothing in between because it was a duplicate. I rang Whetherbys to try and find out more information. I told them facts I had found out on the internet, like he was at Doncaster spring 2008 sales and was un-sold. I asked why he didn't race. I was told he trained as a two-year-old and was pulled from training due to injury. Maybe that is what that big scar/white hair on his front cannon bone is. The RSPCA called me about him and asked to see me for an interview and take photos of the horse. I agreed and gave them copies of the proof of purchase, and photos I took when I brought him.

They commented how if they had seen him he may not have been saved.

They took current photos and took a full statement from me.

Twelve

I decided on Boxing Day that he would have a bridle on and put him on the lunge line to see what he was like; only for a couple of minutes each way. He was so good he dropped his head to have his bridle on. I placed a saddle cloth on his back and fastened a cersingle. I put some pro neoprene boots specially brought for him to support his cannons and fetlocks, also prevent any brushing. I led him to the school and he happily trotted round without fuss.

As his back, where the saddle would go, was almost better, I decided in the New Year it was time to have a sit on him. Others were dubious as to my methods, but I was going to do it in my own time in my own way, like I have with so many young or frightened horses before him.

I got his tack and spent a while in his stable getting him ready, no rush, praising him with every adjustment I made, God bless carrots.

Once we were ready I led him out to the school and walked him around. I knew he was fine with the bridle as I had taken him for walks in it up the track.

On the second day I followed the same quiet process, tacking him up, praising him. I walked him around the school, led him up to a block and raised myself over his saddle just leaning over his back to start, he didn't move so I got off, walked him around constantly praising him, approached the block and stood on it next to him. Okay, foot in stirrup and I'm sitting on him. What a good boy!

I continued with his treatment and taking him for walks underfoot. I now knew he would let me ride him, there was no need to get on him again until I felt he was ready. He developed a sense of humour as he got better and a nose for carrots. I discussed him with the yard groom and yard owner; we felt maybe he would benefit from having some of his coat clipped off as he still wasn't allowed to sweat and it would make treating his skin easier. Out came the clippers, for his first clip he was a good boy, again.

As he was a good boy we went to my car on the way back to his stable where he found and helped himself to carrots.

Rocky pulling the strings

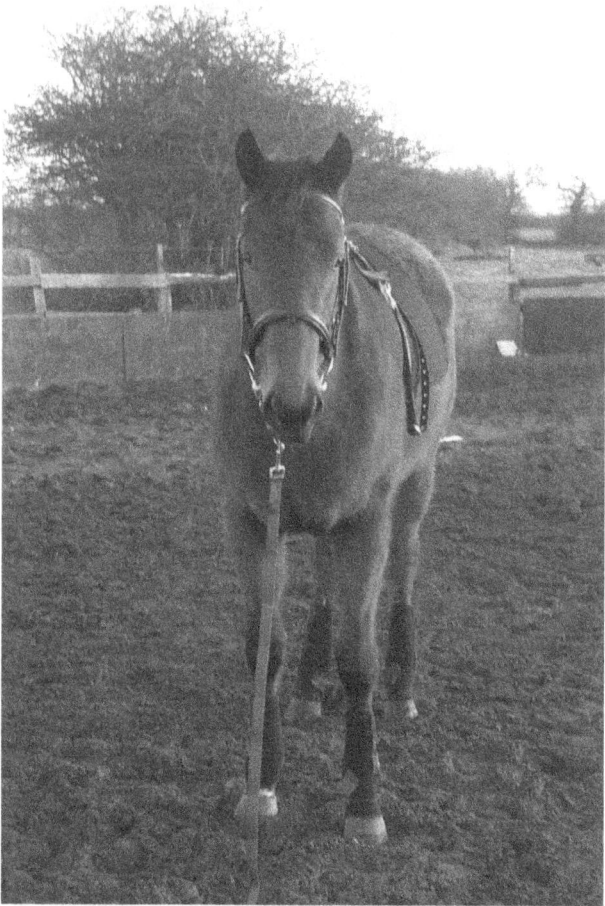

Rocky has developed a liking for the camera

Best friends Rocky and Michelle

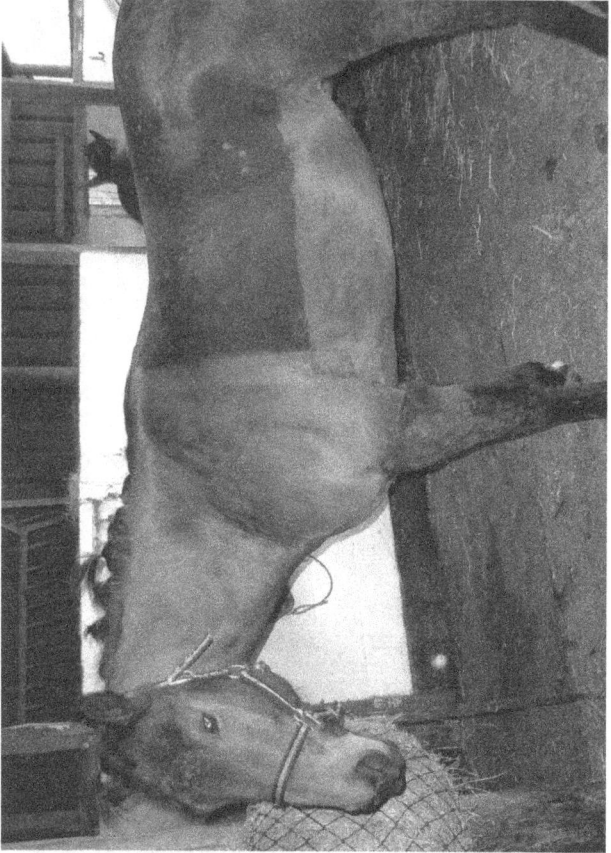

Rocky in relaxing mode and of course, more time to pose for the camera

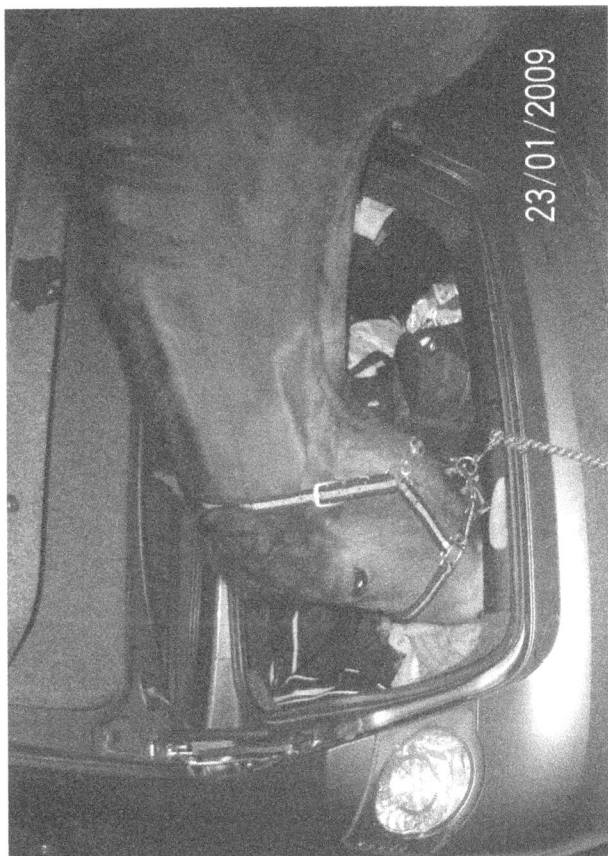

23/01/2009

Cheeky boy! Stealing carrots from the boot of the car

Thirteen

By end of February 2009 he was feeling much happier and healthier. We had been playing in the school and bonding; he would follow me anywhere and everywhere.

My life, still being up and down personally, I had also had to move back into the house I jointly owned due to circumstances. This meant I was living approximately 25 miles away from Rocky again.

By Mid march 2009 I felt he needed to do a little bit of work to start to build and strengthen his muscles, so tack was back on as like in the school, he stood well, he would follow me—no issues.

I got on in the school and we were away of up the track.

The looks on other people's faces that I was going out alone on this young horse was amazing but I trusted him, and felt he trusted me.

Although we were now gently hacking out in just walk, I still kept up his play time in the school as he got stronger the more he played. His personality and character developing, he would follow me around the school whilst gently nudging me for carrots, checking my pockets. I encouraged him to follow me in walk and trot and used carrots as a reward; this was our bonding time.

As spring was nearing an end and we had access to turn out again he went out to have a wander. But he had to be out on his own so he didn't hurt himself, or get chased by other horses as he would try and be playful with them; his skin was still fragile and would split easily.

By May 2009 he was strong enough to be turned out in the field with some friends, where he would nuzzle other horses and sometimes be cheeky and nip them in a playful manner. It was good to see him out with other horses instead of having to be isolated.

He was still out during the day and in at night, he finally left the set of three stables and moved into the big barn with all the other big horses, hunters and liveries. He loved it in there, he could watch everything and everyone.

He loved being in his stable, especially at night, he would wait by his field gateway to be brought in. I think due to his neglect and previous time left out in a field it had some kind of psychological effect on him and he got some reassurance and comfort from being in his stable. He never kicked his door at feeding time but started to nod his head up and down over the door in anticipation of getting his tea. He would put his ears back whilst eating and move his feed bucket away from the door. I think this is so no-one could take it away from him. If I tried to move his feed bucket he would tip it over onto the floor and continue to eat his tea off the floor. He never showed any malice or nastiness with his hay or hard food, which I found quite surprising, it gave me encouragement that he was a kind horse after all he had been through. I was glad he moved into the big barn as his friend, his neighbour in the set of three stables, had started biting him over the wall; through jealousy I think as the other horse was a DIY livery and I was often asked to muck him out by his owner and I would groom him and sometimes ride him. The other horse liked the attention and affection. His owner didn't always make it to the yard everyday so I would fuss him and Rocky every time I went to the yard. Rocky never minded sharing my time with his friend as Rocky was a kind hearted horse. People sometimes say some dogs look like and act like their owners; I wonder if horses are the same.

I was told by other horse owners there they had been worried about him one morning as he was making a funny noise and laid out flat, it seems he snores very loudly.

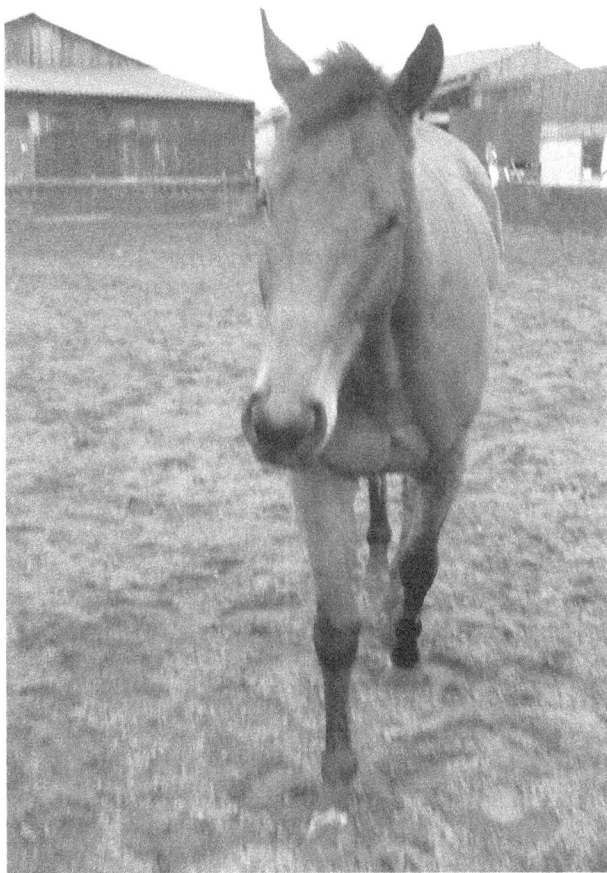

Windswept and interesting

Rocky enjoying the fresh air on his back

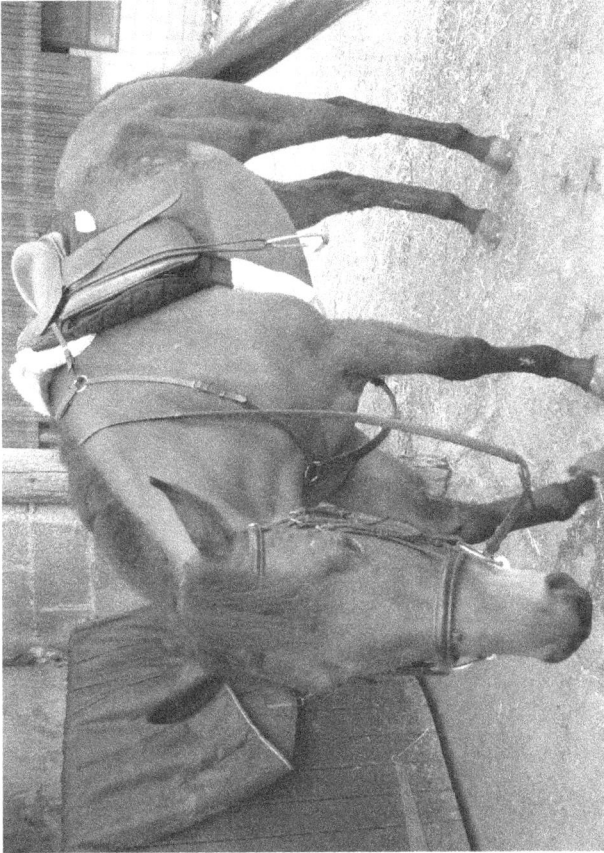

Confidence continues to grow as Rocky gets saddled
up. Rocky is ready to rock!

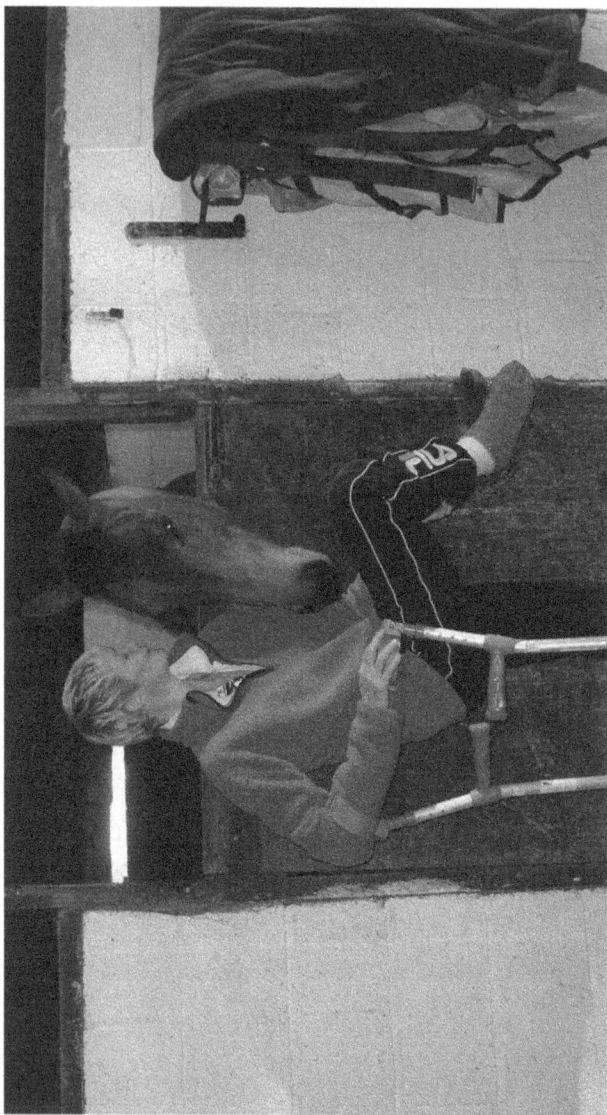

Rocky curious about Michelle's injury

Springing into action

Time to sniff out some nourishments

Rocky mingling with other horses

**Home sweet home. Rocky can't resist another gaze
into the camera**

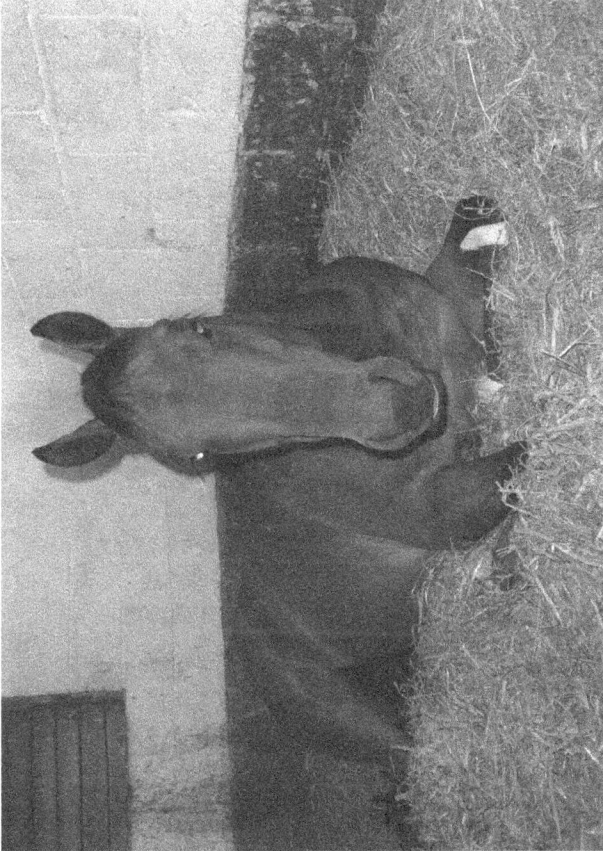

Time to hit the hay! Rocky having a deserved break

Fourteen

I spent the summer getting him fit. Hacking out alone, or with others. He was good to hack out, great in traffic; on one occasion I remember one of the hunters not wanting to pass a stack of straw bales covered in tarpaulin; Rocky went straight past it, then we had to go past a combine—once again the hunter stopped and wouldn't pass it. It started going sideways, but Rocky just kept walking on without even blinking an eyelid as we passed it.

He continued to have the rest of the summer days out in the sun, always coming in at night, he was a happy horse.

As autumn was coming and he had a fine summer coat and days were getting damp, he had to be wrapped up as he was still not allowed to get wet. I think he likes being all snug and wrapped up; his skin was still fragile and sensitive against the rain. I wasn't prepared to risk him getting rained on.

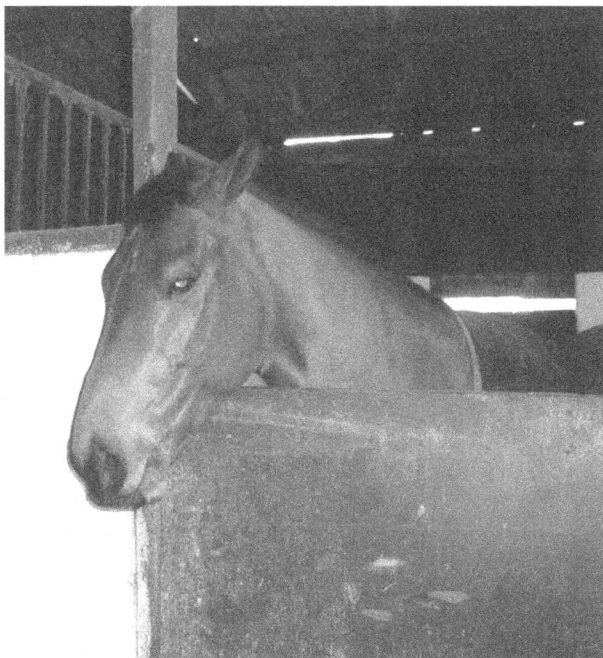

Rocky feeling safe and secure

Snug as a bug in a rug

Fifteen

Winter soon came round again. He was fit and very well, very hairy, so time to be clipped again. This time full hunter clip and *wow,* my stunning boy appeared.

He was ready to go cubing. Now, I am not one that hunts to catch foxes but because it gives us access to galloping freely around the countryside and great opportunity to meet new people, so I got up early, got him ready and went with the yard owner on a Tuesday morning. He was totally fantastic, he didn't pull, kick, he wasn't bothered by the hounds or the horns, he was very polite and stood when asked as cubing is a lot of standing around. To see him you wouldn't have known it was his first experience. I had already decided I wouldn't be jumping him due to his stifle problem and a vet in the summer said it will be doubtful he would ever jump.

Whilst stood relaxing, grazing, and watching—mesmerised by the hounds that were going through the hedge lines—a pheasant flew up and brushed past Rocky's face; which startled him; he jumped sideways. As I had no stirrups or rein contact with him I slipped down one side of him, my left hand was holding onto his knee, my right calf and ankle was on top of my saddle, I was certain looking down at the floor, I was going to end up there head first. I saw no way of righting myself and getting back up into the saddle from this position. Although it seemed ages it was only seconds and Rocky had stood perfectly still whilst I was in this predicament. I stayed calm trying to think how to get back up or whether to except the situation and try to fall gracefully as I could to the ground. Not wanting to scare Rocky or cause a loose horse situation, I was determined I would get back up in the saddle. With that, Rocky seemed to do some kind of movement that I can't explain but it enabled me to push/pull myself back up into the saddle. At no point did I feel frightened. It was as if he knew I wasn't where I was suppose to be. We carried on the rest of the morning without any further incidents. Rocky seemed to enjoy his new experience taking in all the sights and sounds; he also liked it when I would lean forward and give him a polo. He started to learn to bend his head round to my arm, but only when we stood and I offered him one. I still took him for his walks, he was like an overgrown Labrador.

Recovering Rocky in pose

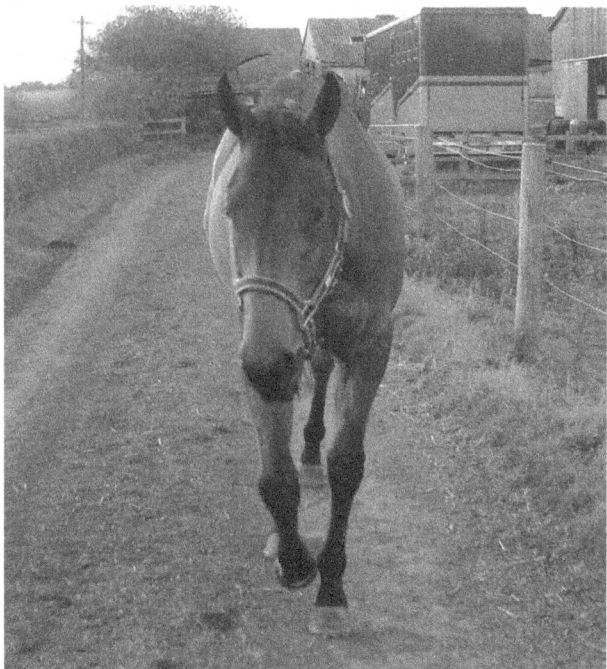

Rocky going for a walk

Sixteen

I was contacted by the RSPCA and informed they would not be able to use Rocky's case against the man I brought him from as apparently I didn't get a vet straight away when I saw him; that I was possibly going to be looked into for neglect. I was so angry and cross at being told this, just because I didn't ring a vet on the first day I saw him I could face prosecution!

I explained the circumstances and information I was given that he had been seen by a vet; that I tried contacting vets but I got no information from the vets. I tried to validate his being seen by a vet. That Rocky, staying on the previous owner's yard, made it difficult to get a vet out to him as I was told to get the previous owner's consent. My priority was to get the horse fit to travel and move him off that yard and away from that man ASAP. Once he was at the new yard he was seen and treated by vets. The horse needed slow increase on food and water before any medication, in my eyes.

Seventeen

Winter was then finally here. We had not turned the horses out since end of September due to all the rain as the owner didn't want the fields churning up, but we could turn out in the school whilst mucking out was done, and/or the horses could go on the walker.

Rocky loved the walker and on one occasion he got out of his stable because the door hadn't been bolted. He took himself to the walker, as time went on and he was going on the walker regularly; he started a new trick that was to lift the flap and panel in front of him up with his head and push—making the panels move faster; hence all the other horses had to move faster. It was decided he would only go on the walker if the yard owner was there and the space in front of him had to be empty. There was a phase where the yard owner was away working and the new groom on the yard refused to put him on because of his sense of humour. I didn't mind so long as he got out of his stable in the school to stretch his legs as the roads were icy so no hacking out. Then the snow came and he went out to play.

Winter Rocky

Eighteen

2010 started very icy but I went with others from the yard to the New Year's day meet in the local town; where we stood for an hour then trotted around roads that had been gritted. Once again he was very well behaved. Happy to let others go in front.

We had a good time and he was very well behaved. Time to head back, get his tack off, oh, and for him to search my pockets for his polo.

More snow came and we couldn't ride but that was okay we still played in the school and he loved his bonding time.

The winter seemed to go on forever. Snow and ice but eventually we thawed out; it was time for the closing meet, which would be his first real meet. I still wasn't wanting to jump him, well, we hadn't really done any proper training over fences as when playing in the school I would lead him over poles and fences but at first he shied away from them — clearly scared. Wow, someone really had frightened this poor little horse. I would have my work cut out if he was ever going to jump which is something I love to do. Show jumping and cross country, nothing better than going fast flying over fences in open fields. The closing meet March 2010, once again he was well behaved.

But he wanted to be up in the field with all the other horses, going fast so for a short time I let him run with the others. Then he noticed the small ponies; he seemed to love the little ponies, he was fascinated by them and was reluctant to go past them so I let him stay at the back with them for a while, which I felt was good for him as it was showing he had manners and would go anywhere in the field.

He was soon tired after a couple of hours. Time to head home. He didn't mind leaving the other horses, think his mind was on his hay net waiting for him at the box. I was so proud of my little horse.

Rocky enjoying some snow

Rocky enjoying warmer weather

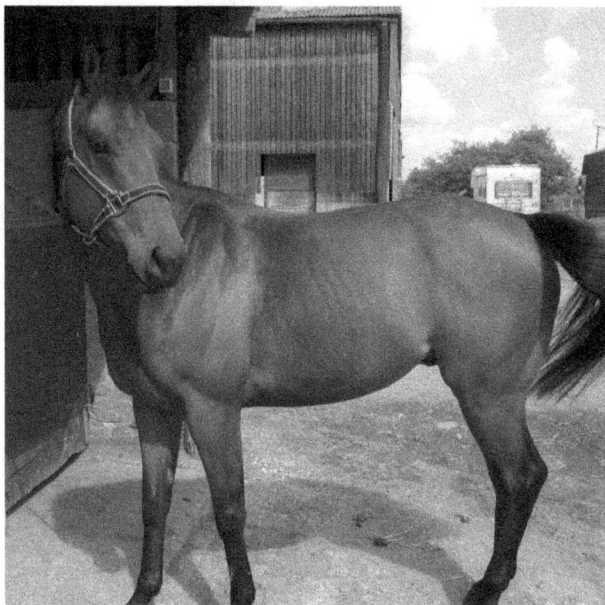

Rocky in striking pose

Beautiful boy! Rocky posing for the camera...again!

Rocky on the search for grass

Strength, power and poise

Nineteen

As it was now April the horses were allowed to go out in the field once again, so I gave him a few days off to chill relax and reflect on his achievements. I was then off the second week of April and time for serious work and some schooling as he is now 5-years-old after all. He didn't like schooling but did so grudgingly. I hate it too, I don't like dressage and have decided he doesn't like it either but he must have basic schooling. He really hated it, so to make sure he wasn't in pain, he was booked into to see a back specialist who checked his back and his saddle. The back specialist checked out his flexibility which was good. He had a minor sore on one side of his back which was massaged out; she checked his stifles which were not so good; which I knew but she gave me some exercises to do with him to build his muscles up. I was advised to use draw reins, an aid I have never liked using but they would help his condition which we have all concluded was sustained by injury and neglect.

He then saw a horse dentist. He had to have his teeth rasped as one side of his molars were sharp. The dentist mentioned for a thoroughbred he has very straight symmetrical teeth which was pleasing, it was also to my knowledge his first experience with a dentist. Once again he was nicely behaved. Some horses strongly object to having their teeth rasped, but then I think I would as well as it appears barbaric to watch but very necessary.

Due to circumstances I had moved again into a

bungalow. The bonus being it was only a mile to Rocky's yard. It meant I had to travel to work but I would rather live close to Rocky and travel to work some 30 miles than the other way round. The house I jointly owned was gone forever, so no risk of ever having to move back there or have to share again. I had the Westies living with me; I now had a perfect home close to Rocky. I would get up 05:30 to walk the Westies before going to work and no matter what time I finished work I would take the Westies to see Rocky on a night.

I received a letter from a solicitor, stating they were acting on behalf of the RSPCA so I contacted them and told them what the RSPCA had told me. He apologised for their actions and informed me I would be required and did I have photos and all the original paper work, which I confirmed I had, the solicitor again apologised for the miss understanding and stated Rocky's case was very important due to all the evidence and photos I had taken and collected. The case was going to court the trial had been set for 2011.

Now we had the all clear from the back specialist and the dentist; the schooling started again.

Once we had mastered basic schooling I wanted to introduce some poles. Rocky was clearly frightened of the poles as he would shy away from them in the school when riding around them. I thought this strange as out on hacks he wasn't scared of anything so before I could ride him over poles I thought I would result to a favourite tactic of mine I had previously used to get young or nervous horses to walk over poles and learn to jump. I got off him, I started walking round the school moving the poles whilst he followed me, I gave him carrots to encourage him that he was safe and this was a fun thing to do, not scary. I then placed four poles evenly spaced out that I wanted him to walk over. I walked over them and he followed. At first he sniffed them and tripped as he didn't pick his feet up high enough but this exercise would be great for his stifles. After a couple of times following me and carrots, I got back on him and we rode over the poles.

I knew Rocky would follow me; especially if I had carrots in my pocket. When we had mastered ground poles I put some very small fences up, little cross poles only approximately 8-inches high, to start with so he could have walked over them, I was taking him right back to basics.

Every time I put a new fence up I would jump off him and go over it on foot with him following me, giving him lots of praise. It wasn't long before I could put new jumps up or put same jumps up but in a different area of the school and he would go straight over them so we progressed to going to a little local show in the summer and bless him, I took him in the clear round which we trotted round, but still new place; never seen a course with me before. The clear round is a class you can go in to practise jumping a course, it is not a completion against others. He didn't shy away from the different coloured fences or knock any down so we went in the smallest novice class and bless him, double clear he came forth.

First show out so proud of this little horse. Previous owner and vets said he didn't, couldn't, wouldn't jump. Well we have proved them wrong!

We spent the summer hacking, schooling, and raising the jumps just a little, playing in the field and school.

He started getting bothered by the hot summer flies so I got him a new rug which I thought was fun.

He also started to have a habit of sticking his tongue out which I found to be very cute and funny.

I started teaching him to allow me to carry things whilst I was riding him. I would ride round the school moving the cones, carrying a shield, or a lance, getting him used to different things. I put a trick saddle on him and stood up, sat back to front on him, he must think I'm daft but anything I want to do with him he lets me. We did some drill work with the other horses that were practising for a show they were due to do.

The yard that he is at does an assortment of skills, jousting, cavalierly skill at arms, hunting, trick riding, driving, riding lessons, filming, the opportunities are endless.

I would do little bits with him I had seen others do with the trained horses in the hope that maybe one day he may be able to do something exciting. He went well in the second row with a pole used for tent pegging; shame his mum couldn't get the end of the pole on her boot.

So we had a great summer learning so many new things, he was keen to learn and quick too. A friend at the yard also had a young horse so we hired a local school with jumps to practise and get the horses off the yard.

He was so excited at the surroundings, very keen

and fast, to slow him down I turned him towards one of the higher show jumps we hadn't lowered for our training, to my surprise he flew over it, it was at least 3-foot high with a 3-foot spread, a big coloured fence. It was if he was trying to prove a point; he was excited—almost showing off! I felt he was bored of little fences.

So I decided we would go to the last local end of summer show. Once again we did the clear round. By now he knew what he was doing and decided to get slightly excited and go fast. We went clear, but I decided to put him in the novice class despite his high spirits. Wow, we went clear, okay now the jump off to do; I didn't think we could go any faster, see the photo for the outcome.

He won his class although small fences; it was only his second ever show. Now remember, this is the little horse that would never jump!

Rocky sizing up

Rocky shows Michelle the way

Mission accomplished

Undercover Rocky

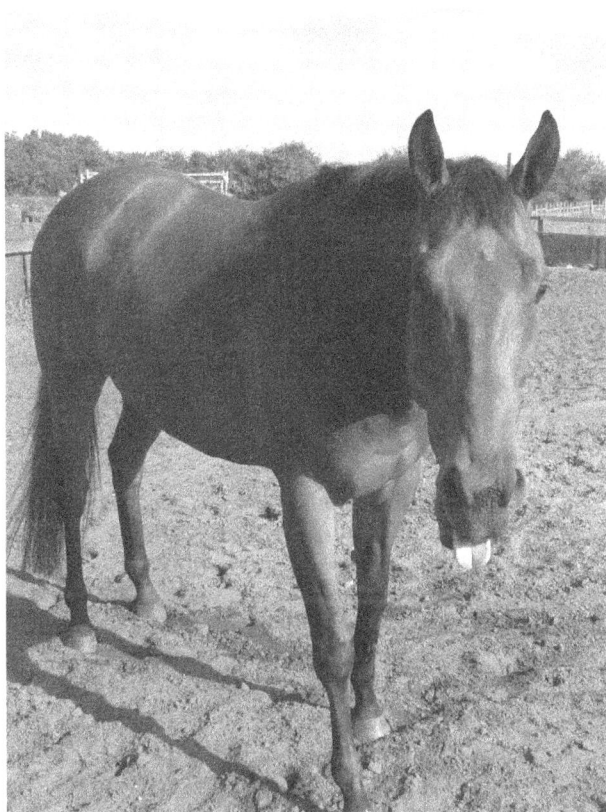

Cheeky!

And...action!

The gathering

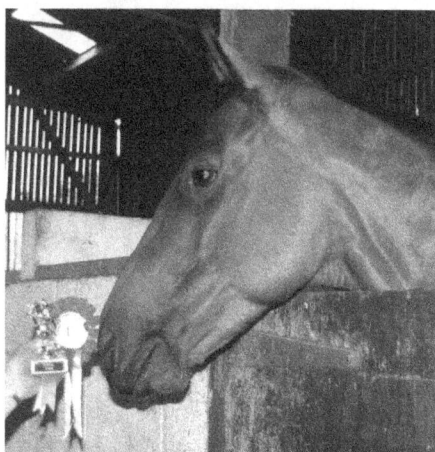

The champion

Twenty

Winter is soon upon us again. I'm moving house once again, to share a house which is closer to work and further away from Rocky but I have a heart and will help others in need. As I was asked to share a house and help, maybe this time will be different, boundaries were set.

I know Rocky is happy, healthy, and enjoying life. He's a right character and I love him to bits.

One damp cold winter's morning the owner of the yard tells me he needs a 16th thoroughbred gelding for a film. Could he have Rocky? "Of course," I said. Do what you like with him as Rocky and I trust everyone at our yard; everyone is friendly, helps each other out, we have a great tea room there. He tells me he will need to do some training, and would go off filming for a few weeks in January 2011.

The yard owner and his son set to work training him. Everyone at the yard helped when it was time to take him in the local Church. What was this film he was going to be in? So I asked and found out it's a book called *Weighed In: The Story of the Mumper.*

When I got home I went online and ordered a copy, it took ages to arrive. His training consisted of being ridden around a cross-country course next to a fake camera on a quad bike. He was ridden in the indoor school with someone holding a broom for a microphone and fake camera. I was told Rocky was very good, he didn't seem phased by anything. I was asked not to clip him again and to let his mane grow as for the first part of the film he had to be scruffy. This was all very well timed in my mind as I had nights at work to do and the roads were thick with ice and snow so I couldn't make it to the yard; much to my disgust as I wanted to see my boy.

The time flew by and it was soon January 4th 2011. The day was here he was off on his filming travels. I arrived at the yard to help get him ready making sure he had everything including first-aid kit and plenty of rugs—well he is my baby and he was going until the 20th January 2011. The yard owner's son was going with him.

As I use the internet and I'm on a social site, I searched the author and found the film's fan page which I instantly flagged I liked. The copy of the book arrived and I read it in three days as I was off from work due to a minor injury. If I was a horse would I be put down or would someone care for me as I do Rocky? So many people in my life have said if I was a horse I would be shot!

I messaged the author of the book and said how brilliant the book was. I didn't let on that Rocky was away filming and was the chosen to be the Mumper. The author replied and I asked if he had any badges left I had seen on the fan page, being my usual cheeky self, but I wanted one for Rocky. The author of the book was putting updates of the filming on his social site and I made a comment much to my surprise he asked if Rocky was mine, as my profile picture was of Rocky's head. I said yes and how the compliments on how lovely and well behaved Rocky is and has been, how everyone loves him. I was told he was doing everything asked of him and the yard owner's son and Rocky make a great team.

They had all heard he had been rescued and did I have pictures of when I rescued him, which of course I have; would I send them to them as one of the back scene camera men wants to do a story/article on him like a documentary: a success story from a neglected rescued horse to the famous Mumper. So I sent the photos.

Whilst he was away I followed his progress and looked at filming pictures. The first pictures I was sent of Rocky as the Mumper with the cast.

When Rocky got home, I went to see him, as I walked into the barn he saw me and whickered, so pleasing to hear I'm still mum, or maybe it was the carrots I was carrying.

When I saw the yard owner's son he told me some stories how everyone spoiled him with treats and who the main culprit was so he was sorry if Rocky goes through my pockets. I just laughed, he told me how he ate all fruit from the cast and crews' pack lunches: bananas, pears, apples, that everyone loved him and he stood on set perfectly when the other horse was all sweated up. He explained some of the shots he had to do and that he enjoyed the galloping. I looked amazed at him as I was told Rocky was only doing the camera shots, there was another horse to do the galloping scenes, but I asked how he was, he said fine, very fast he loved it. I was relieved and okay with it all as I know he was well looked after.

So I was waiting for the rest of the photos, he was due to go away filming again in February to finish of any bits they need. I have been asked if I would let Rocky go to the film premier. Wow, totally amazing! Who would think my little horse would become a film star after his rough start in life? But for now he is home enjoying his stardom.

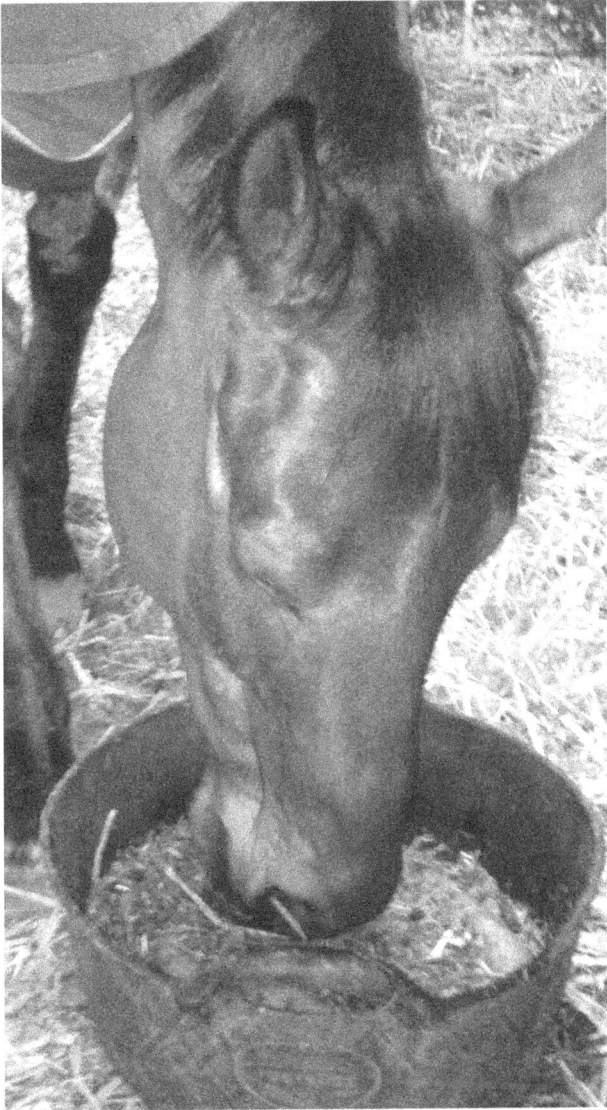

Dinner at Rocky's

Rocky in full swing

Showing off for the camera

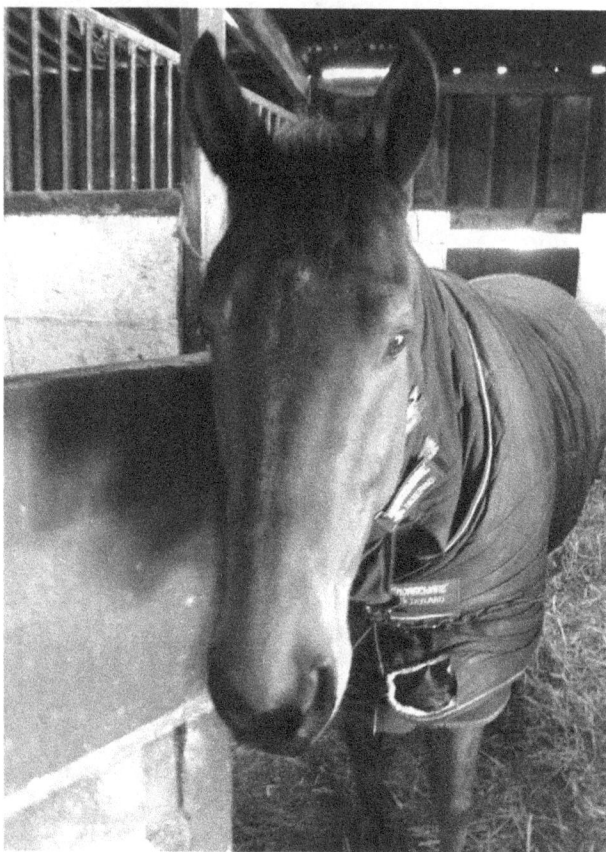

Rocky always makes time for the camera

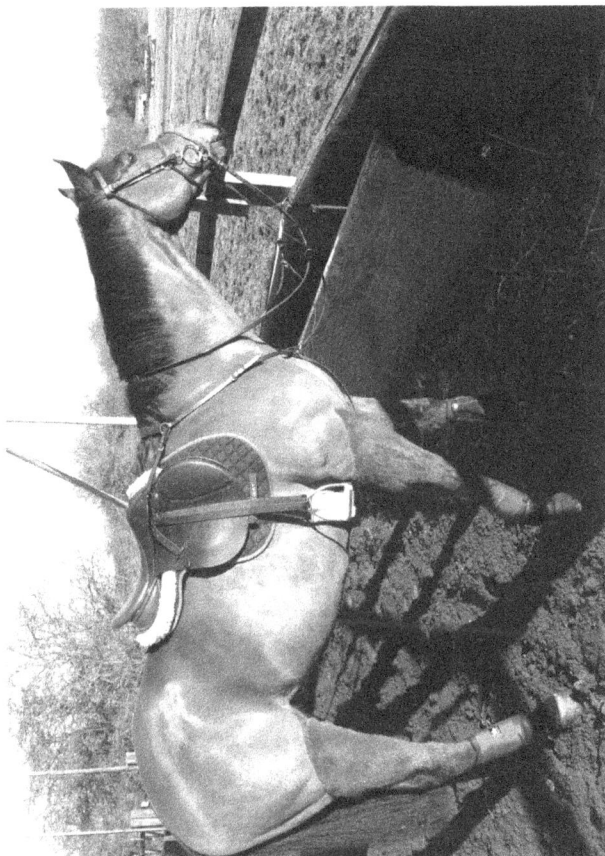

Rocky getting ready to rumble

Twenty-One
January 2011

I was contacted by the solicitor acting on behalf of the RSPCA. He told me the case had been dealt with prior to going to court. That a guilty plea had been accepted, which would save the RSPCA on court cost. I was informed of the outcome, which was pleasing. Some justice for Rocky but mainly protection for future horses and animals. The man was given a five year ban and all animals removed from his care. I updated the solicitor with Rocky's progress as he asked how he was going now. I explained his recent exciting activity and mentioned the possibility of this biography of his life from my rescuing him to film star. He advised me by all means *right* his story but for legal reasons identities and whereabouts of who and where he was found and neglected by must not be named.

The solicitor asked that as this is a clear success story, to be told of any films or documentaries Rocky is in, as he would like to publicise the fact that rescued horses can with the right care survive and go on to live full happy lives. He thanked me for all my evidence and commitment in helping with the case stating it's only people like myself that help the RSPCA bring the right people who neglect animals to justice. Time to move forward; there is closure on the court case. Rocky has justice.

Twenty-Two

I have received some photos of his visit and filming at Epsom. He looks amazing. The feedback I have is, "He was fantastic," "He's fast," and "So well behaved."

Rocky has been enjoying his time back at home hacking out, playing in the school. He is due to go away filming early February 2011 but only for three or four days this time. His trip away filming included a trip to the beach, where I was told he didn't want to go in the sea at first but once someone walked in, in front of him, he followed them then he was away and loved his visit to the seaside.

Everyone on set apparently loved him and I have received lots of praise from people that worked with him during the filming. Here are some of the actual comments sent to me via email and the social site. I was asked to send some photos to someone on set of what Rocky looked like when I rescued him.

<u>Messages from some of the crew. For legal reasons some names and opinions have been removed.</u>

Hi Michelle,
Thank you, for the photos. How awful he looks. He is a lucky boy having you to give him all the TLC he needs in abundance! He has done you both proud, he is an absolute star and I would not hesitate in using him again! He has done everything we have asked of him willingly and with the yards owner's son on board, they are the perfect combination. He has a fabulous temperament too and even my boyfriend who is still wary of horses because of a bad experience in his childhood has fallen in love with him but who could blame him...everyone down here loves him! When he was standing patiently and perfectly behaved in the Church, brought in and held by one of the cast, our 3rd AD said she has worked on horse films for numerous years but NEVER seen a horse so well behaved! There is a guy on set filming 'behind the scenes' and he is keen to do a piece about Rocky and his rise from an abused and neglected soul to fame as The Mumper. I will pass on the photos to him and let you know the outcome.
Take care and thanks again!

Hello Michelle,
Had no idea The Mumper was your horse, my word, lovely. We were with him all day on Wed at Epsom and he was so well behaved, the missus even gave me an apple. We both love horses, so it was lovely to be close up to one, we don't see many in the streets of South London! I have some photos of Rocky I took on Wed, will get them on the social site soon. Best.

Michelle,
I'm a keen collector of horse shoes, done it for years,
getting as much luck as possible! Any chance of getting
one off you from Rocky?

I sent the author of the book a front shoe from Rocky, which he photographed.

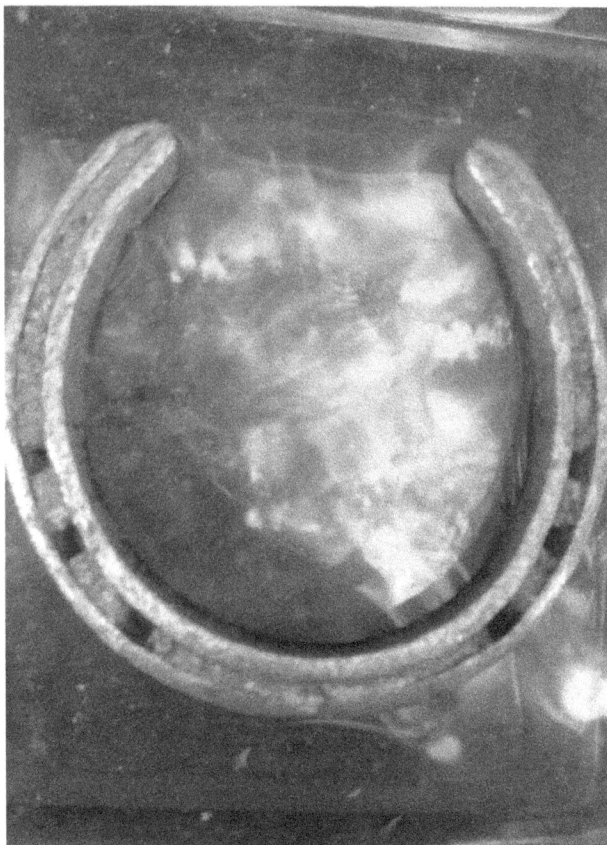

The shoe that fits

Rocky and Michelle preparing practise

Rocky and Michelle

The perfect team

Rocky always has a nose for curiosity

Twenty-Three

March 2011 Rocky has continued enjoying life as I continued with his schooling: he is improving every time he is ridden.

However not long after these picture were taken I had to have a break from riding due to a non-horse related injury. I couldn't ride so I discussed Rocky with the yard owner. I was asked if they could use Rocky for a society who carry out historical re-enactments which I agreed to. He did a couple of displays as a lancer, however he is young and inexperienced so he was only used once on each event but it is all good experience for him.

He has also been used for a select few people who are more advanced in their riding abilities to have lessons on recently, which I don't mind as it is good for him to have other people ride him and it has kept him fit whilst I have been unable to ride.

My life has turned around since having Rocky and this year it's got even better despite having a back injury and not riding. I would still see Rocky as often as I could just to see him and fuss him with my new partner, who I must add has no knowledge of horses and was slightly weary at first, but has over the past few months got to know Rocky, feed him carrots and bonded with him and love him as much as I do. We go as often as we can, we have the house I previously shared with someone else, I ended up taking it on by myself initially but now we share it and I have a perfect home life, however driving the 27 miles to Rocky's yard aggravated my back but I can't not see him, it's like having a dark mass in my head and heart not riding him let alone not getting to see him, so my partner mucks him out or tidies his bed and grooms him whilst I supervise.

Moving him closer to my home is not an option in my opinion, as he is happy at the yard where he is. I can rest and be assured all his needs are catered for when I have to work.

I trust Rocky so much and know he trusts me. One day we tacked him up and I put my partner on him and he followed me round the school being very careful; it was as if he knew he had someone on him that had never ridden, he was so good.

Handsome Rocky

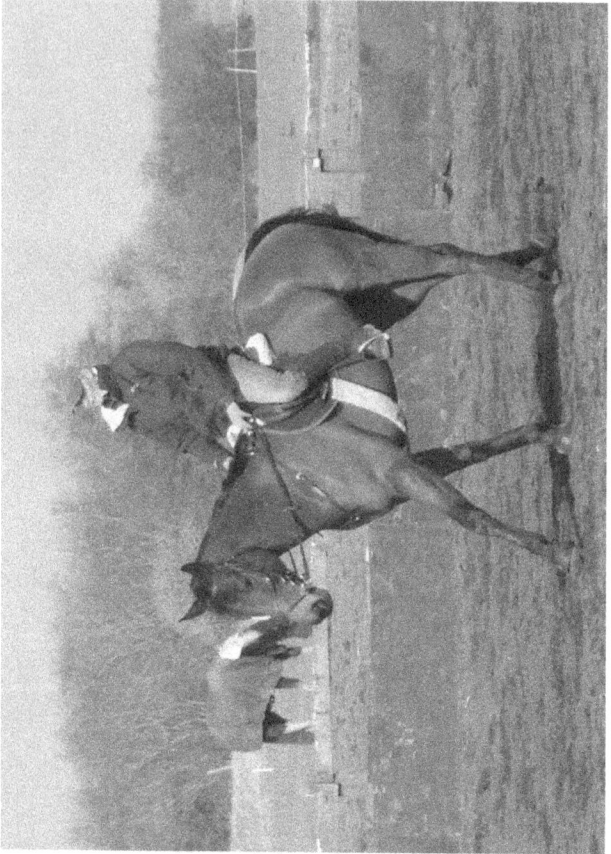

Rocky and Michelle, a match made in heaven

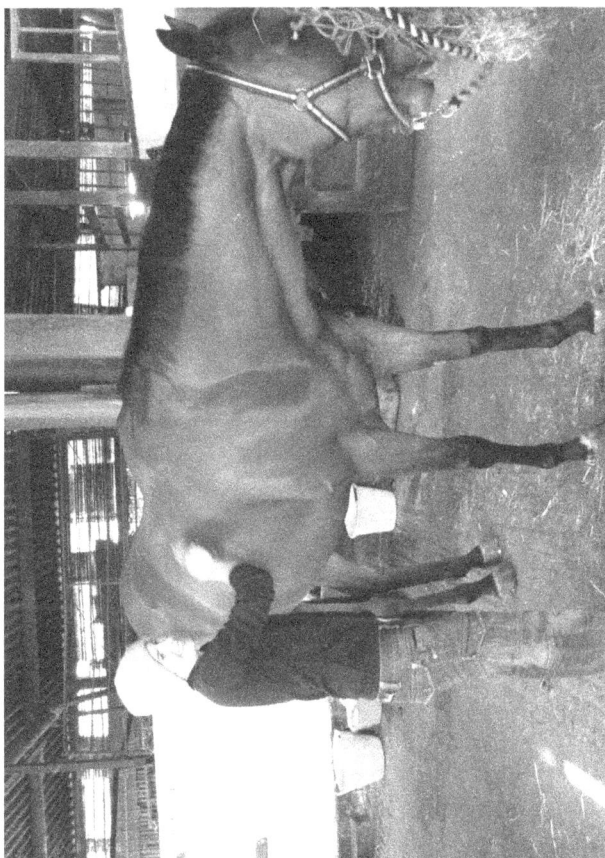

Rocky getting a brush down

Twenty-Four

April 2011 I was contacted by the yard owner and asked if I would do an interview for a documentary the film crew were doing on Rocky's life. As my back was feeling much better I agreed and went to the yard the following day where the interview took all afternoon. I had to explain my feelings and emotions about Rocky, how I found him, why I chose to buy him — all in front of the camera and unlike Rocky: I hate cameras.

The following day we returned for the photo shoot of Rocky. Whilst everyone was at lunch I prepared Rocky, plaiting his mane, my partner brushing him, he loves all the attention and being fussed.

Once the film crew were back and ready we let him out of his stable and he wandered round the yard.

He thought he was off for a ride, so I had to hold him. His little Westies brothers happy to see him; he also had time to meet his little sister; a puppy Westie who is intrigued by Rocky — she loves to lick his nose.

Rocky has two brothers and a sister. They are all Westies and they love going to see him.

I had to walk around the school. Rocky just followed me then he had to do his photo shoot. I thought I was the camera shy one. I found it comical when I saw the photo: we were both looking away from the camera in front of us.

Rocky knows where the carrots are kept

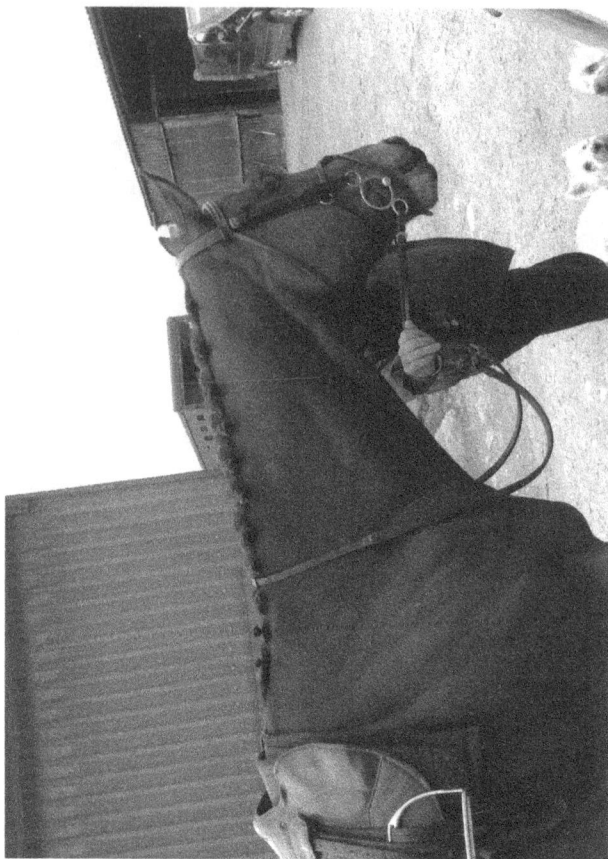

Rocky eyes up the Westies

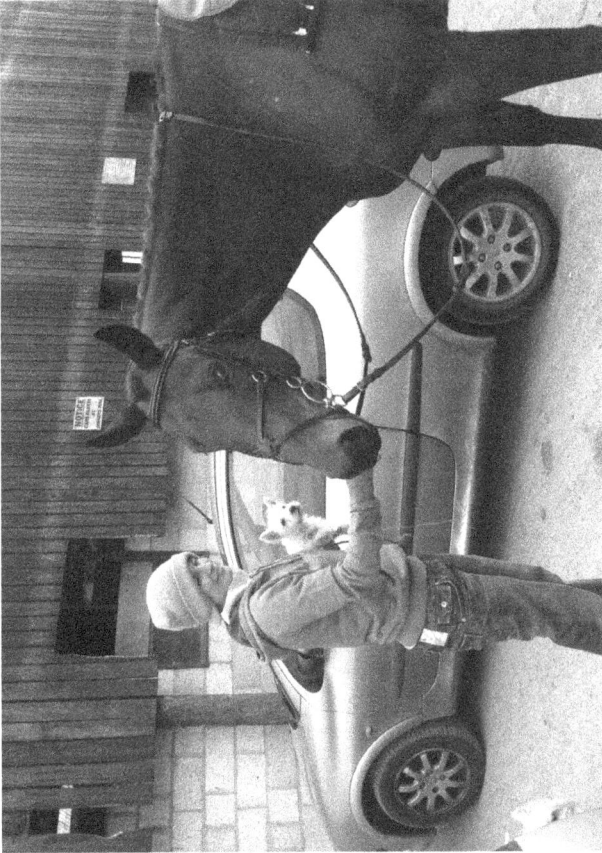

Family guy, Rocky with the Westie onlookers

Rocky and Michelle find a relaxing moment

Twenty-Five

Summer 2011 is upon us. I haven't had much chance to ride as my back was injured again in May, much to my disappointment. I would not be able to take Rocky to any local shows this summer, driving was again aggravating my back and making it worse so once again I had to stop going as much as I wanted to, but I knew he was being ridden and well looked after as a full livery.

I discussed my injury with my partner and we agreed I could go to see him as I couldn't not see him, he's like a child to me, not just a pet but my boy. My partner was feeling the same. If we could he would live in the house. My partner would muck him out or tidy his bed and we'd see him in the field. He would see me or hear my voice and call out to me, whinny or whickers, this has carried on all summer just visiting. Wet days, sunny days, we turned up just to visit him.

One late summer's day the owner of the yard asked would I please sit on Rocky, he wants to use him for a three day trip away to reinact the boar war but Rocky has on a couple of occasions shook his head when ridden by other people when he has been used for lessons.

He was tacked up and I sat on him. I had a little walk trot and canter, he was foot perfect, worked nicely for me, he must have known I was still sore or in some pain as he didn't put a foot wrong and he was so gentle and easy to ride. As he was so good for me, it was mentioned maybe he missed his mum and just need his mum to sit on him and ride him for a bit. It was decided he would go for the experience and the society riders could try him. So he was bathed and got ready for his travels.

What's in it for me?

Mummy's boy!

Rocky steals a moment to pose for the lens

Rocky always on the prowl for treats

Debbie bonding with Rocky

Twenty-Six

We had a family outing, my partner, the three Westies and Rocky. We went camping, blow-up beds and all, despite the torrential rain we had a great time.

On the Friday evening Rocky and another horse were used in a two-horse rifle shooting practise.

I think he was excited. Big open grass field, very fit and feeling well. The rifle was shot and he was off, having a good gallop. Oh dear, the rider did stop him but said he is young and inexperienced so he wasn't going to be used, he looked stunning in the cavalry tack.

On the Saturday I was asked if I minded Rocky going with other youngsters at the back of the Boar war display. Of course I didn't mind. The rider was, in my eyes, a good considerate rider and he asked me whilst tacking up what's the best way to ride him and asked me for any useful advice. I just said, "Reassure him, talk to him, and relax on him." Off he went, happy to be out of his paddock joining in.

The rider told me he was very good. Just young and needs experience. He didn't fire rifles of him but they stood near by the rifles and cannons being fired. This was another great experience for him.

On the Sunday before he was due to go home I rode him in the practise area just so he could get to be close to the action on the other side of the hedge. The gun fire, the other displays going on, he was very good—very alert. He walked past people in different costumes. He was very good boy. We walked, trotted, cantered, and just stood watching the goings on over the other side of the fence: a massive confidence boost for him. I wanted him to realise big open spaces doesn't mean time to go fast. I had spent a long time at the beginning of riding him walking him on grass verges and tracks educating him that just because we're on grass doesn't mean he can gallop. With me on his back he didn't even try and gallop off. I call myself a lazy rider at time because I'm so relaxed and ride with long reins which I feel helps him to relax too.

We had a fantastic weekend. 05:30 morning walks for the Westies, trying to sneak past Rocky's paddock but he would hear me calling the boys if they went too far a head of me and Rocky would call to me and wander to the fence of his paddock and wait for me to go fuss him so we visited him and gave him a polos.

Rocky wasn't allowed to sleep in the tent with us but I bet he would if he could and was allowed but there wouldn't have been any room for anyone else on the blow-up beds as it was the Westies on a night snuggled in under the duvets to keep warm.

So to sum up Rocky's life and the small glimmer I once saw in his sad eyes nearly three years ago, my trust, hope, risks have all paid off for us both as I have a loyal outstanding brave little horse that gives me so much pleasure and unconditional love. Well it costs me a few carrots, polos and aniseed imperial sweets but I am content and happy in the knowledge justice has been done and this little loving kind horse has a happy secure loving home and family for life with a promising future full of prospects.

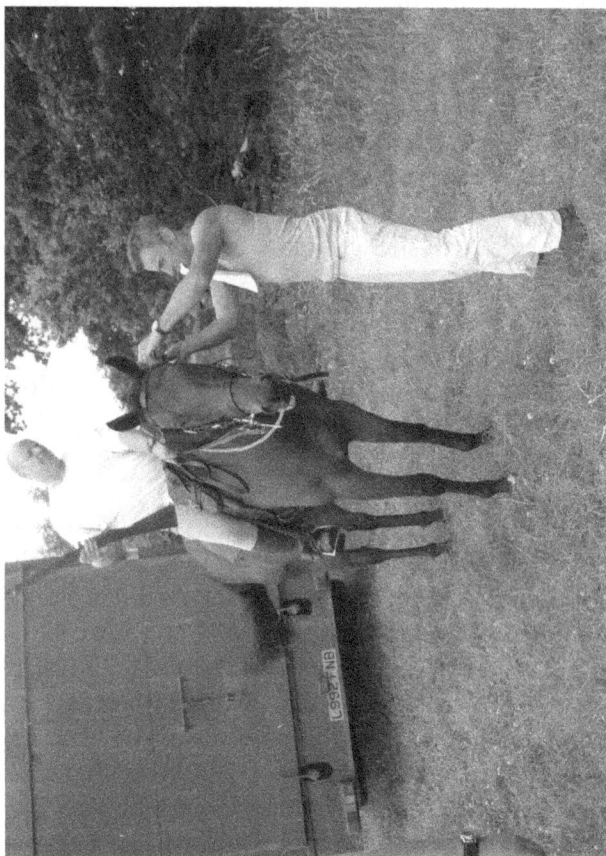

Getting ready for rifle practice

Rocky leads the way, he's off like a shot

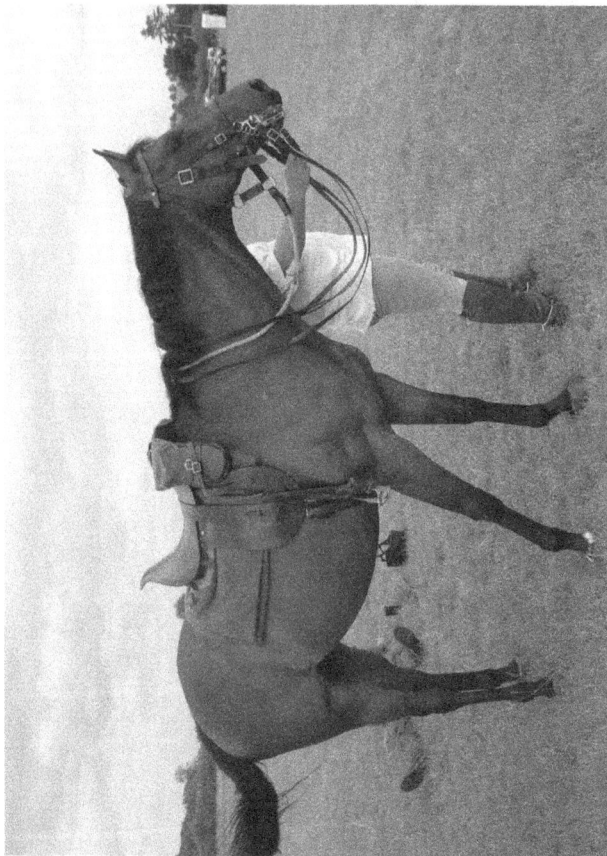

Dressed and alert

Here's looking at you, kid!

Rocky leads the way to the Boar War

Rocky and Michelle in the wide open space

Unconditional bond

Low sky, high spirits

Rocky loves those camera moments

To some expert riders my position is not text book style, but it's my way of encouraging and helping youngsters over fences safely. Plus, I'm off his back and it's got him jumping when he's stopped lots of times.

I like horses to move freely under me without being jabbed by the bit whether they jump or not and with Rocky; he was so unpredictable you couldn't tell if he was going over until you were over as he could do the approach then let you think he was going to take off but stop dead etc.

I did have a laugh seeing the pictures, as it looks like Rocky is jumping a 3-foot fence. Not bad considering just a pole on the floor would make him run away a few months prior to the following shots. But now he flies round courses, flies over hunt jumps and when I'm well again we may start doing cross-country as he's so clean at jumping and loves going fast.

Up! Up!

Flying without wings

Very proud Mum

Becky gives Rocky much-deserved treats

April 2009

New Year's Day 2010

New Year's Day 2010

New Year's Day 2010

New Year's Day 2010

March 2010

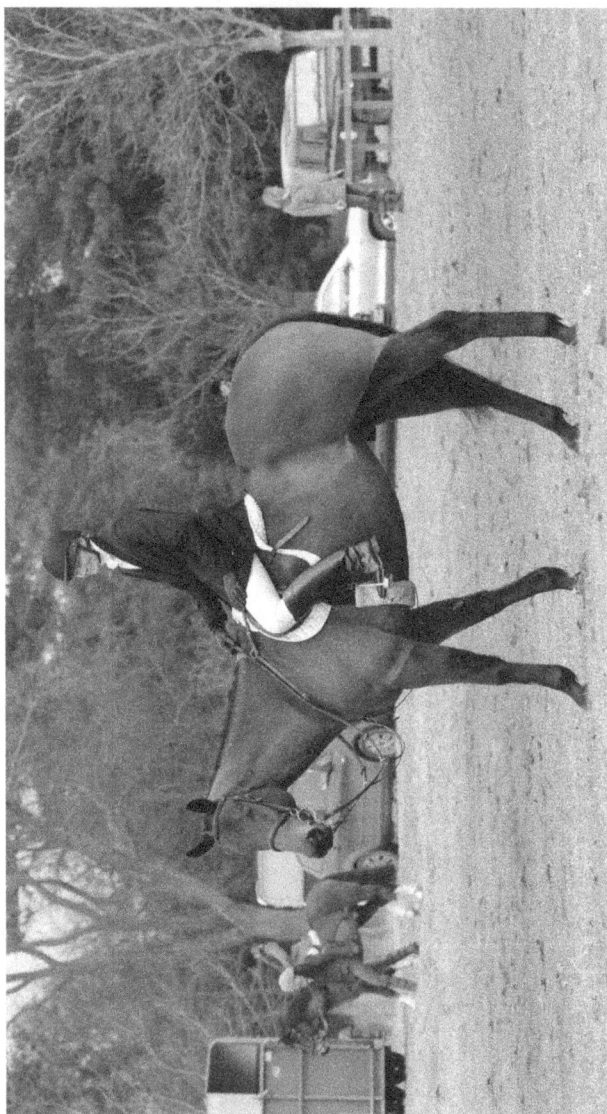

March 2010

Rocky's Acknowledgments

Rocky wouldn't be where he is today without the help and support from the Atkinson family and their staff aka Atkinson Action Horses. Rocky loves living at your yard and is very happy.

Special thanks to Mark Baxter and Paolo Hewitt and their book, *Weighed in: the story of The Mumper.* This has given Rocky a chance in a lifetime to star in a feature film which has led to a documentary being made about his rise from a life of neglect to fame as *The Mumper.*

Author's end note

I would like to thank Mark Baxter for sending me the brilliant photos of Rocky on the film set. Unfortunately, due to technical problems detached from our control, some photos never made it into this book but nevertheless, my huge thanks to Mark.

Special thanks to all who have helped Rocky on the road to recovery.

Great thanks to the film crew and cast.

My appreciation for those who gave Rocky a fighting chance.

A Glimmer of Hope: Rocky's Story
by Michelle Brown

Featuring Rocky, many people who have helped,
and special guest stars.

Publication by SHN Publishing
www.shnpublishing.com